Theory and Practice of Administrative Reform

Editor and Author
Koji Yokoyama

Authors

Koji Hirose

Akiyuki Sannomiya

Kazuo Kondo

Ryota Hirose

Akihisa Hirata

Taketo Shima

Translator

Yosuke Morizono

SUNRISE

Preface

These chapters on administrative reform were written and compiled at the beginning of 2023 as the nation entered its fourth year since the onset of the COVID-19 pandemic in early 2020. Theories abound as to the COVID-19 crisis, with optimists touting its end and doomsayers convinced of its continuation, and today we find ourselves living in an era of uncertainty, unsure of which narrative to believe.

Yet even in these challenging times, many municipal employees are diligently addressing various administrative tasks, ranging from the pandemic response of local governments to adapting to new digital transformations (DX). I deeply respect their efforts and dedication.

Occasionally, however, one might observe municipalities and their staff persisting with outdated ordinances and systems with no attempt to modernize. Relying on precedent and convention is no longer viable, especially in this unprecedented era of population decline and super-aging society. Like living organisms, administrative management must continuously adapt to changing times.

To support administrative management reform, Shiga University has been offering the Administrative Reform Workshop since the 2019 academic year, targeting municipal officials and local council members. The program provides insights, skills, and expertise in administrative management.

This book has been revised and enhanced for publication based on keynote lectures given by instructors of the Administrative Reform Workshop. It encompasses cutting-edge topics indispensable for administrative management reform, from the significance and methods of reform to financial analysis through public accounting, municipal DX, BPO promotion, and public enterprise and facility management.

It is our sincere hope that many municipalities will navigate this era of uncertainty with strength, facilitated by genuine administrative management reforms. We would be honored if this book can aid in that endeavor.

March 2023
Edited by : Koji Yokoyama
Professor of Economics at Shiga University / Director of the Social Collaboration Center

Table of Contents

Preface

Chapter 1

Why Is Administrative Reform Necessary Now?

Declining Population and Super-Aged Society / National Financial Difficulties / Public Infrastructure Crisis / Expansion of Administrative Functions and Dysfunction of Existing Organizations / Public and Private Role Allocation / Changing Concept of Public Affairs / Consequence of Not Implementing Administrative Reform

Chapter 2

What Is Administrative Reform?

Lineage of Administrative Reform in Japan / Legal Basis of Administrative Reform / Regional Revitalization and Administrative Reform / Flawed Administrative Reform / Procedures for Administrative Reform

Chapter 3

Comprehensive Plan and Administrative Evaluation

Introduction / Development of the Comprehensive Plan / What Is the Comprehensive Plan, and Its Significance / Formulation Status of the Comprehensive Plan / Frequently Asked Questions / Development of Administrative Evaluation / What Is Administrative Evaluation? / Status of the Introduction of Administrative Evaluation / What Are Evaluation Indicators? / Examples of Common Mistakes in Evaluation Indicators

Chapter 4

Policy Formulation and Administrative Work Review

Introduction / What Is Policy? / Elements of Policy / Elements of Finance / Clarification of the Policy Decision-Making Process / Revisiting Policy / Revisiting the System and Style of Administrative Operations

Chapter 5

Financial Analysis Based on Local Government Accounting (General Accounting & Public Enterprise Accounting)

Introduction / What Is Local Government Accounting? / Explanation of Financial Documents in Local Government Accounting / Units of Preparation and Their Effects / Historical Background and Necessity of Local Government Accounting / Main Financial Analysis / Concerns of Fiscal Insolvency and Cost Rigidity / Profit and Loss Statement by Purpose / Public Enterprises / Sections Requiring Business Management Skills / Current Situation of Deficit Compensation / Conclusion

Management Resources) / Management Related to Things / Management Related to Money / Management Related to People / Conclusion

Chapter 1

Why Is Administrative Reform Necessary Now ?

Shiga University, Koji Yokoyama

Declining Population and Super-Aged Society

This paper aims to address the pressing question of "Why is administrative reform imperative at this juncture?" In my assessment, there are five predominant factors, with the first and foremost being the nation's dwindling population coupled with an intensifying super-aged society. This dynamic pervades every facet of Japan's contemporary social and public policy challenges. Japan first saw its population decline in the 2015 census, and the 2020 census confirmed that the population's contraction and aging trend are accelerating. While municipalities confronting the issue of depopulation display evident concern, certain regions flanking JR lines continue to grow and portray a misplaced lack of urgency. Notably, such growth is largely confined to high-rise apartments or emerging residential zones proximate to train stations, leaving the peripheries grappling with persistent depopulation and societal aging. Current projections anticipate that by 2040 every prefecture will register a drop in population compared with the 2010 statistics. By 2060, the aggregate population is expected to be approximately three-fourths of its current size with the aging rate nearing 40 percent. Alarmingly, numerous local governmental bodies appear nonchalant with no proactive interventions in sight.

Evidence substantiating these observations can be discerned from the statement by the Ministry of Internal Affairs and Communications on April 1, 2022. According to the Depopulated Areas Reflecting the Results of the 2nd Year of the Reiwa National Census, predicated on the Special Measures Act for Sustainable Development of Depopulated Areas (commonly termed the New Depopulation Act), 885 municipalities can be classified as "all depopulated," "partly depopulated," or "assumed depopulated." Given that Japan encompasses 1,718 municipalities in total, this reveals that a majority are grappling with depopulation. This statement also supports the Japan Revitalization Conference's 2014 declaration, estimating that 896 municipalities will potentially cease to exist by 2040. Though there is a discrepancy in the denominator and prerequisites compared with the 2013 data (1,799), approximately half the municipalities are depopulated or teetering on the brink of extinction. The conundrum, however, is not the abrupt vanishing of these areas, but the incremental difficulty of upholding government administration, social security, and employment structures. The "boiled frog theory" serves as an apt metaphor, illustrating how imminent threats manifested gradually often go unaddressed until it is too late. This ostensibly mirrors the predicament of present-day local governments. Even with the population crisis looming large, there seems to be an overarching reticence to spearhead reforms, with some municipalities, as per available information, already incapacitated in certain sectors due to personnel deficits. The exigency for administrative reform is undeniable.

While numerous local governments are instituting migration, settlement, and childcare support strategies as pillars of regional revitalization, the efficacy of these measures, in the face of overall demographic shifts, may be tantamount to a mere drop in the ocean.

Among elected officials, including mayors and council members, we see a subset pledging to invigorate urban areas or to commission new infrastructure, yet they notably omit discussions pertaining to the anticipated population decline during their tenures. Such an approach might be characterized as lacking strategic foresight. It is imperative for governance to make judicious determinations encompassing compact urban planning, subsidy reassessments, and regional community reinvigoration, especially in light of the looming challenges posed by our shrinking population and increasingly aged society.

The salient point I wish to underscore is not to adopt a bleak perspective toward the impending demographic shifts and pronounced aging of society. Instead of fixating on increasing the population or enticing migration from different locales, our focus should pivot towards urban planning and public policy adaptations that harmonize with a demographic reduced to three-fourths of its current size. This pivot would encompass recalibrating public infrastructures in terms of physical assets and re-evaluating extant organizations and initiatives in terms of their operational dynamics. The objective is to sculpt a societal framework and system where individuals can lead fulfilling lives, even with constrained fiscal resources and a population reduced in size. These strategies epitomize the "administrative reform" which I will discuss in this volume.

While we have examined macro-level population dynamics, there may be some who find it challenging to relate to the situation personally. Let's therefore delve into a more micro perspective, focusing on the number of employees within local governments. The Japanese populace often harbors a strong reliance on government, believing that even if the population dwindles and communities collapse, causing various societal functions to stagnate, local government offices will ultimately step in to assist. As a citizen I share this sentiment to some extent, but being well-informed about the current realities, I am also aware this may not always be the case.

The number of employees in local public organizations across Japan in 2022 has decreased by approximately 480,000 (or 15%) from its peak in 1994, and it is likely that staff numbers in many municipalities have dropped by nearly 20 percent. Yet, the staff workload has not diminished and continues to increase. I suspect that numerous local government employees are overwhelmed, to say the least. Japan's bureaucratic structure, including the central government in Kasumigaseki, can be described as being in a precarious state.

One might wonder when the decreasing number of local government staff becomes most problematic. The answer is during such emergencies as natural disasters. In recent years, we have seen a surge in natural calamities like torrential rains and earthquakes, causing widespread damage almost annually. One of the significant challenges during such times, although seldom highlighted by the media, is the hampered functioning of local government offices, which is no surprise given the decreasing and aging workforce. It is implausible for municipal staff to visit each household on rescue missions during times of disaster. Thus, there is an undeniable need to clearly delineation of roles between the public and private sectors. Citizens must also take the initiative and assume responsibility for tasks within their capabilities. And this is not limited to disaster preparedness. In all policy domains as we move forward, residents must recognize the inadequacy of sole reliance on administrations, as even local government offices might become incapable of rendering assistance. This does not imply that the government has no role to play, however. Appropriate role-sharing between the public and private sectors, citizen collaboration, and public-private partnerships are crucial. I will elaborate on this topic further on. The primary takeaway from this section is that both local government employees and residents must contemplate future urban planning and public policies against the backdrop of a declining population and super-aged society.

National Financial Difficulties

The second factor, and it goes without saying, is the nation's precarious financial state. According to announcements from the Ministry of Finance, the long-term debt balance of the national government and regions reached an astonishing 1,223 trillion yen at the end of fiscal 2021, which equates to a debt of roughly 9.7 million yen per citizen. Around the mid-2000s, when the debt hovered around the 600 trillion-yen mark, there were fears that the country would become insolvent, prompting mergers of cities and towns during the Heisei era. The debt has since doubled and is now equivalent to twice Japan's GDP, the worst among developed countries. No other country faces such a dire situation. While this level of debt might seem too immense to fully grasp, the October 1 consumption tax hike in the first year of the Reiwa era is a glaring testament to the poor state of the nation's finances. With the onslaught of the global pandemic in early 2020, national expenditures have only increased, and the long-term debt continues to grow. There are concerns about the increasing burdens on local governments, which must now strive for the soundest finances possible.

Delving deeper into this fiscal quagmire from a granular perspective, one must consider the financial anatomy of local governments. Various metrics are used to gauge the fiscal vitality of a municipality, but the most revealing is the general account expenditure-to-revenue ratio that compares essential outflows, such as personnel compensation, subsidies, and bond expenditures, against principal revenues like local taxation and routine local allocation taxes. A ratio proximate to 100 percent signifies fiscal inflexibility. As of Reiwa 3 fiscal year, the national mean for municipalities stood at 93.8 percent, indicating that discretionary budgets in these jurisdictions are constricted to minuscule margins. This slender allowance is for the most part pre-allocated, leaving negligible leeway for discretionary allocations. Promises of extensive initiatives by aspiring mayors and council members are often rendered, but they simply attest to a clear disregard for fiscal realities.

What delineates the fiscal landscape of your local government? I am privy to certain municipalities teetering on the precipice of the 100 percent threshold within the next two to three years. The repercussions of the COVID-19 pandemic could potentially hasten this trajectory, and breaching the threshold would inevitably mean a curtailment in personnel expenditures. I was aware of various municipalities resorting to this measure during fiscal 2020. This recourse, however, is a manifestation of managerial desperation rather than strategic reform. While this situation might be tenable for elected officials, the workforce grapples with broader existential considerations. Deteriorating occupational conditions, devoid of any systematic overhaul of superfluous public amenities and subsidies, will further debilitate municipalities and culminate in diminished services for the populace.

Therefore, I earnestly entreat municipal personnel to champion administrative reforms preemptively. Concurrently, it is my aspiration that citizens transcend parochial regional affiliations and entrenched interests, embrace a holistic understanding of municipal governance, and eschew perpetual reliance on public infrastructures and subsidies.

Public Infrastructure Crisis

Third, even amidst these strenuous fiscal challenges, the cost burden of municipal finances most heavily relates to public infrastructure expenditures.

According to the Ministry of Land, Infrastructure, Transport, and Tourism, by around 2033 many public facilities and infrastructure will exceed 50 years old. It is not just aging, however, but also the diversifying needs of residents and users and the demands for improved accessibility, earthquake resistance measures, and other services that will necessitate significant renovations and upgrades. Another estimate from the same ministry projects that, by the latter half of the 2030s, maintenance and renewal costs will surpass the total investment amount. This means that municipalities may not have the budgets for new infrastructure developments, but will be incessantly chasing after maintenance and renewal. All of this is anticipated to unfold within the next decade or so.

In anticipation of these challenges, the Ministry of Internal Affairs and Communications has ardently advocated that all local public entities institute a Comprehensive Management Plan for Public Facilities, and assiduously advance with sound stewardship of these public assets. Yet, have we not seen numerous local jurisdictions exhibit tepid advancements, often stymied by entrenched regional and group-centric predilections? I fervently hope that mayors, council members, and the general citizenry will make judicious decisions and avoid passing on fiscal liabilities to subsequent generations.

Correspondingly, the oversight of public enterprises remains a locus of concern. Consider water supply services. Certain municipal projections intimate that, under the current trajectory, their financial reserves could be depleted within a matter of years. The sustainability of water supply services in some municipalities is teetering on the brink, evolving into a national quandary. Newly inaugurated zones may benefit from contemporary infrastructure, whereas older regions confront formidable challenges. Consequently, the Ministry of Internal Affairs and Communications is exhorting public utilities encompassing water and sewage systems to delineate "management strategies" advocating judicious tariff recalibrations and methodical upkeep. Further, legislative modifications to the Water Supply Act and the PFI Act in late 2018 sanctioned a concessionary framework, wherein public institutions retain asset proprietorship, but operational mandates are delegated to private sector entities.

While facilities associated with funeral rites and waste management have made advancements through enhanced regional collaboration, analogous measures are indispensable for utilities such as water and sewage systems. This principle extends to other public amenities as well. The future will see individual municipalities finding it increasingly arduous to sustain a comprehensive package of public facilities and infrastructure, making an expansive regional outlook even more imperative.

It is paramount throughout this transformative process that public services are not compromised. Equally, it would be inimical to the principles of equity if only facilities in regions with pronounced advocacy endure. Local administrative bodies bear the responsibility of elucidating to their legislative assemblies and general populace, the prospective fiscal outlays related to the renovation and administration of public amenities, the strategies ensuring equitable regional dissemination, and the methodologies under consideration — be they amalgamations, unification of services, privatization, or other mechanisms — all in the pursuit of fiscal stability.

Expansion of Administrative Functions and Dysfunction of Existing Organizations

The fourth factor relates to the expansion of administrative functions and the dysfunction of existing organizations and programs. Throughout my career I have reviewed administrative projects across numerous municipalities, and have frequently come across programs from obscure organizations that disbursed subsidies, which in today's context would be difficult for residents to understand. These subsidies often trace back to initiatives introduced during the Showa era, making them relics from a time of financial affluence. When did the bloating of administration commence? I pinpoint its origin to the high-growth period of the late Showa 30s. In essence, rapid economic growth furnished abundant financial resources, paving the way for a surge in legislation and comprehensive public policies and the expansion of administrative functions. This growth was sustainable when financial resources were aplenty, but as funds dwindled, a critical reevaluation of the priorities and necessity of certain administrative functions became imperative. The real concern is that policies and programs conceived during the high economic growth and population boom periods remain unchanged in today's era of declining population and resources. If anything, the number of administrative projects has escalated, setting municipalities on a visible path to administrative bankruptcy.

Another pressing concern is the dysfunction of existing organizations. In recent times, there has been no shortage of news detailing improprieties in regional organizations established in the post-World War II period. Misappropriations of membership fees by local community association and PTA leaders, unjustified trips disguised as inspection tours by welfare commissioners, coercive membership into community associations and PTAs, and excessive subsidies and entrenched vested interests in socio-educational groups are issues that surface repeatedly.

Certainly, the majority within these organizations are dedicated to their missions. However, irrespective of the group, most grapple with declining memberships and dwindling resources due to population declines and aging demographics. It is not uncommon to find cases where the core mission of an activity is lost, with the sole objective becoming the survival of the organization itself. Moreover, there are numerous instances where these entities have morphed into convenient tools for fund collection and mobilization for higher administrative bodies.

At the heart of these issues lies the fact that postwar established entities are ill-equipped to tackle modern-day challenges, rendering them dysfunctional. Perhaps it is time to earnestly contemplate whether we should reorganize, merge, or reinvent these entities to meet current demands. With limited resources and manpower, it is crucial to assess which community challenges to prioritize and determine the most fitting organizational structures to address them.

Public and Private Role Allocation

I would like to consider the expansion of administrative functions from a different perspective. Historically, up until the early modern period, Japan primarily operated based on a model of civic and local autonomy. The Edo period, for instance, witnessed local community leaders like village headmen and influential landlords overseeing local governance. Following the Meiji era, with the establishment of a modern administration, administrative structures matured and arguably overly expanded by contemporary standards. From the early 2000s, there has been a growing emphasis on citizen collaboration. This does not imply a simple reduction of administrative functions. Rather, it suggests a need to reevaluate the division of roles between public and private sectors to avoid potential gridlocks.

A fitting example is disaster prevention where the emphasis is on public assistance, mutual assistance, and self-help. There are tasks best suited for governmental bodies, those that individuals should undertake, and efforts demanding collective neighborhood action. For instance, individuals are responsible for their own evacuation and preparation of emergency goods. For tasks beyond an individual's capacity, community cooperation, such as assisting its vulnerable members, becomes essential. It is also crucial for local governments and residents to collaborate on creating individual evacuation plans. On the other hand, responsibilities like establishing evacuation centers or mobilizing the Self-Defense Forces lie exclusively within the purview of administrations. This is not a matter of shirking responsibility from public to private sectors or vice versa. By each entity effectively assuming its appropriate role, the overall disaster preparedness of a community can be enhanced.

The delineation of roles is not exclusive to disaster management but is requisite across all administrative sectors. Within administrative bodies there are many instances where the essence of citizen collaboration is misconstrued. It is often observed that only the departments responsible for collaboration actively promote it, leading to collaboration for collaboration's sake. It is imperative to refine the division of roles between public and private entities across all administrative domains. While this will be elaborated upon in Chapter 15, it is a fallacy for administrations to assume responsibility for all public matters or, conversely, for everything to be borne autonomously. A shift in perspective is required from both administrations and residents.

Changing Concept of Public Affairs

And fifth, I believe the concept of public affairs itself is changing. In recent years, the term PPP (Public-Private Partnership) has become increasingly popular, whereas NPM (New Public Management) was commonly used before. NPM was a trendy term from the late 1990s to the 2000s, and in contrast to PPP, NPM directly translates to "New Public Administration." In essence, it means incorporating private business methods into local government management. This concept originated in the United Kingdom and influenced the development of systems in our country, like the Designated Administrator System and administrative evaluations. However, these approaches were considered insufficient, so recently the concepts of PPP, including PFI (Private Finance Initiative), Designated Administrator System, private consignment, and outsourcing have been promoted. The ultimate goal of PPP is for both local governments and private entities to fully take on the public domain. In our country, PPP mainly focuses on the construction and management of public facilities and is far from its true form.

Furthermore, in 2011, the concept of "collective impact" was introduced by John Kania and Mark Kramer of the U.S. company FSG Consulting. Collective impact is defined as "a commitment made by a group of key players from different sectors, gathered to resolve a specific complex social issue."

Taking these global trends into account, the Ministry of Internal Affairs and Communications' Local Government Strategy 2040 Research Group's Second Report (2018) made proposals on what local governments should be like in 2040. Reading this report, I feel it resonates with the concepts of PPP and collective impact. Until now, local governments have been service providers, meaning providers of public services = government offices, which is a given in Japan. However, from now on, local governments should serve as platform builders. In the future, private companies will provide public services in each policy field, whether it is welfare, education, or others. If the public domain is a platform for public services, the role of local governments will be that of a platform builder. The research group of the Ministry of Internal Affairs and Communications suggests this is the direction to take. It is difficult for me to imagine such a world truly coming in the next 20 years, but local government employees and we citizens may be on the verge of a major paradigm shift.

Consequence of Not Implementing Administrative Reform

I have mentioned five points as to why administrative reform is necessary. If we fail to implement administrative reform, the consequences are clear: ① Limited administrative staff and resources cannot sustain public policy; ② Communities and organizations in regions lacking support and funding cannot be maintained; ③ Mistakes in administrative processing will increase, leading to staff fatigue and interpersonal troubles; ④ Contemporary issues such as severe social withdrawal, lonely deaths, DV, child abuse, special fraud, and shopping refugees will not be addressed; and ⑤ Worst of all, no reform will lead to such scandals as embezzlement and falsification of public documents by officials from residents' associations, PTAs, social education groups, welfare groups, and administrative staff in charge. Ultimately, the failure to implement reform may result in a decline in public services or even municipal bankruptcy.

Administrative reform clearly cannot wait, and the demands have only increased with the COVID-19 crisis. With the current crisis, measures like ① suspension of non-essential events and projects, ② simplification and digitization of documents and procedures, ③ promotion of telework and reduced working hours, ④ suspension and shortening of non-essential meetings, and promotion of remote work, and ⑤ promotion of private sector vitality are now being implemented. But these are reforms that should have been made before the crisis. Reform should not be something done only during a crisis or end when the crisis is over. That said, any crisis should be seized as a great opportunity for reform. We must "turn misfortune into fortune" and utilize the COVID-19 crisis as an opportunity for reform.

Summary of Chapter 1: Various factors including population decline, super-aged society, national fiscal difficulties, administrative expansion, and changing public concepts call for administrative reform. However, the biggest issue is the fatigue of existing postwar organizations and businesses now unable to address contemporary regional challenges. Local government management involves supporting the public domain through appropriate public-private collaboration. In light of the COVID-19 crisis, I believe we should further advance administrative reform.

References

※National Institute of Population and Social Security Research, "Total Population and Age Structure Coefficient: Medium Birth (High Death) Estimate" (2018)

※Ministry of Internal Affairs and Communications, "2020 Census: Basic Population Statistics" (2021)

※Edited by Hiroya Masuda, "Local Extinction" (Chuo Koron Shinsha, 2014)

※Ministry of Internal Affairs and Communications, "Special Measures Act for the Sustainable Development of Depopulated Areas: Overview" (2022)

※(Note 1) The definition of "Municipalities at Risk of Extinction" refers to cities, wards, towns, and villages where the population of young women aged 20 to 39 is projected to decrease by more than 50% between 2010 and 2040. Additionally, 523 municipalities with a population of less than 10,000 (estimated) in 2040 are regarded as "highly likely to vanish." The regional requirements under the new depopulation law include a population decrease of 30% or more from Showa 55 to Reiwa 2, a financial capability index of 0.40 or lower resulting in a 25% or more decrease, and an elderly population ratio of 38% or more.

※Ministry of Internal Affairs and Communications, "2022 Local Public Entity Staffing Management Survey Results" (2022)

※Ministry of Finance, "Japanese Fiscal-Related Materials (April 2022)"

※Ministry of Internal Affairs and Communications, "2022 Local Government Finance White Paper (Fiscal 2020 Financial Statements)" (2022)

※Ministry of Land, Infrastructure, Transport, and Tourism, "Current and Future State of Aging Social Infrastructure" (2018)

※Ministry of Land, Infrastructure, Transport, and Tourism, "Land, Infrastructure, Transport, and Tourism White Paper" (Fiscal 2009)

※Ministry of Internal Affairs and Communications, "Local Government Strategy 2040 Concept Study Group - Second Report" (2018)

※David Peter Stroh, translated by Riichiro Oda, supervised by Kayoko Nakakoji, "Systems Thinking for Social Change: A Practical Guide" (Eiji Press, 2018)

Chapter 2

What is Administrative Reform ?

Shiga University, Koji Yokoyama

Lineage of Administrative Reform in Japan

In Japan, the term "Gyokaku"—short for administrative and fiscal reform—has in recent years expanded in its connotation. In this volume, barring cited references, it is largely synonymous with administrative management reform. The term rose to prominence during the Nakasone Cabinet era, marked by the privatization of three public corporations, Japan-US structural adjustments, and other significant shifts. Subsequent cabinets continued this trend: the Hashimoto Cabinet ushered in central government reorganization and local decentralization strategies, followed by the well-remembered Koizumi reforms. This period also saw the evolution of the Trinity Reforms and the Heisei municipal mergers. Under the Abe administration, PPP policies were in the forefront of Abenomics. Beginning in fiscal 2020, the fiscal-year employment system was introduced, and internal control frameworks became obligatory for prefectures and major cities. Presently, initiatives such as digitalization are gaining momentum. While not exclusively crafted for administrative overhaul, I regard all these measures as integral to the administrative reform trajectory.

It is a common misconception that administrative management reform primarily targets cost reduction. Yet, Masami Hiraishi has articulated the three discernible trends of "fiscal reconstruction and small government," "market and deregulation," and "governance reform." When we examine these trends within the context of local governments, the fiscal reconstruction and small government principle is evident—it mandates limiting the administrative scope and curbing fiscal outlays. But administrative reform transcends this dimension. The market and deregulation facet emphasizes a shift from an exclusive reliance on administration to more liberalized market engagement. This evolution is manifest in public-private partnerships and community alliances, evidenced by mechanisms such as the Designated Administrator System and PFI. The final governance reform arguably holds paramount significance as it necessitates an overhaul of governance structures and encompasses facets like regional autonomy and transparent information-sharing protocols. It is imperative that we recognize administrative reform as multifaceted, because beyond fiscal prudence it embodies the infusion and rejuvenation of private sector dynamism, systemic enhancements, and governance evolution.

Legal Basis of Administrative Reform

At the national level, the goal of the Administrative Reform Promotion Act is to realize a simple and efficient government, with the "basic philosophy" of administrative reform expressed in Article 2. Article 3 states, "National and local public entities have a duty to promote administrative reforms in accordance with the basic philosophy in the next chapter to realize a simple and efficient government." However, most provisions relate to national reform and few concern local public entities.

Relatedly, the Government Policy Evaluation Act targets national administrative agencies and does not regulate the policy evaluation of local public entities. Therefore, local government approaches and attitudes toward reform vary.

Local governments do not conduct administrative reform without a basis, however. The Local Autonomy Act, considered the constitution of local autonomy, refers to "democratic and efficient administration" in Article 1, and "minimum expense for maximum effect" in Article 2. There are also clauses on "rationalization of organization and operation, and proper scaling." Thus, local autonomy itself is inseparable from administrative reform.

While phrases about minimum expense for maximum effect, and rationalization of organization and operation," leave little room for interpretation, democratic and efficient administration can be interpreted in various ways. One interpretation warns of a loss of democracy in the pursuit of efficiency. Relying solely on majority rule, for example, is efficient but not democratic. Another interpretation is that a healthy democracy requires efficient administration. Governance undermined by irregularities or scandals, especially financial, will ultimately falter. Such organizations are often autocratic and lacking in democratic governance. Hence, I believe that regularly operating an efficient and appropriate organization ensures a democratic administration.

Other laws related to administrative reform include the Act Concerning the Fiscal Soundness of Local Public Entities and the Financial Soundness Act. Moreover, many local public entities have established administrative reform guidelines. The initial request for such guidelines arose during the Nakasone administration, followed by demands during the 2000s related to the enactment of the Local Decentralization Law and Heisei municipal mergers. Words like personnel management, organizational restructuring, and privatization were common. Many local governments still operate under the guidelines from this era, so there is a need to update these guidelines to fit contemporary times.

Regional Revitalization and Administrative Reform

As I mentioned earlier, administrative reform includes governance reform beyond cost-cutting. When each department undertakes administrative reform, the culture of the entire organization begins to change. I can generally tell which local governments are likely to experience misconduct; they are usually the ones where basic administrative tasks are performed improperly. Furthermore, I believe the ultimate goal of administrative reform is the reform of local communities. Local governments provide subsidies to communities and organizations, but there are many cases where they continue to do so despite ongoing misconduct, unable to stop due to various entanglements. Administrative reform includes rectifying these issues. It is about reforming the entire town, including both the local government and the community.

In relation to local communities, I am often asked about regional revitalization, as I have been appointed as a "Regional Revitalization Evangelist" by the Cabinet Office's Regional Revitalization Promotion Office. Therefore, I would like to touch upon regional revitalization as well.

The first phase of the regional revitalization strategy (2015–2019) has ended, and the second phase (2020–) has begun, but I do not think the first phase was evaluated particularly high. Its biggest flaw, in my opinion, was its over- reliance on external transfers, whether economic relocation (tourism policies represented by inbound tourism, corporate inducement, etc.) or population relocation (migration and settlement policies). The current pandemic has inadvertently exposed these issues. Looking at the second phase of the regional revitalization measures that started in fiscal 2020, the focus remains on the over-concentration in Tokyo, an idea devoid of novelty. While the promotion of telework should certainly be advanced, transfers from the outside cannot be entirely negated. However, the sentiment that "those days were better" with "plenty of people and money," so "let's return to that state," does not represent true regional revitalization, in my view. In a world facing population decline and fiscal difficulties, real regional revitalization lies in reviewing organizations and businesses to suit the current era as well as in carrying out reforms to make organizations, businesses, and ultimately, local communities, resilient in a time of dwindling population.

For instance, while migration and settlement in rural areas are being promoted, and corporate relocation is encouraged, are local areas truly prepared to welcome people from the outside? There are stories of people who have moved to the countryside only to be ostracized and subsequently return to the city. Also common are stories of corporate workers who transfer but do not integrate into the community before moving on again.

It is important to break down non-democratic traditions to ensure that new residents can live comfortably as they settle in and come to love their new hometown. Both old and new residents need opportunities for learning how to better understand their town and the system of civic collaboration that encourages active participation in town planning.

In terms of tourism, the focus should expand beyond creating new tourist facilities or adopting the strategy of desiring what others have because it was successful elsewhere. Rather, regional revitalization should involve shining a light on the historical resources and natural features buried in the region and polishing them as new tourist attractions.

Regional revitalization often garners attention for its feel-good stories, but the true goal is to build a democratic community where everyone can live happily with limited personnel, budgets, and resources. This aligns with the purpose of administrative management reform.

From the above points, I believe the following four are important in summarizing administrative reform: 1) Administrative reform is not solely about fiscal reconstruction and small government, but also encompasses markets, deregulation and governance reform; 2) The essence of local autonomy is based on the perspective of administrative reform; 3) Administrative reform is not just about cost-cutting or reform within government offices; it is also about reforming the entire region, including local communities; and 4) The first step in regional revitalization should be the revitalization of local government management.

Flawed Administrative Reform

I would like to discuss the procedures for reform, but first I want to examine the issues related to reform. Local governments implementing reforms may be using the wrong methods or the reforms may be hollow and ineffective. The problems are countless, but here I would like to identify reform from six major perspectives.

1. "System & Structure" perspective: The mechanisms for administrative evaluation and reform have not been established. Organizations promoting reform such as administrative evaluation committees are not set up. External experts are not involved in the reform process. Tasks ranging from comprehensive planning to administrative evaluation are not systematically undertaken. Reform is not linked to budgets, personnel, or other administrative matters.

2. "Method (Phase-by-Phase)" perspective: (By phase I mean each step of reform, which I

will explain in the next section.) A master plan for reform has not been formulated. The content of the reform master plan is hollow and not regularly reviewed. An inventory of tasks (understanding the amount of work) has not been carried out. A review of administrative projects has not been conducted. The review of administrative projects is not performed separately by revenue and expenditure, region, and organization. Regular administrative evaluations are not carried out or are wanting. Administrative evaluation sheets are complicated and burden the staff. Proper evaluation standards for administrative evaluations have not been set. Appropriate evaluators are not appointed.

3. "Public Facilities & Other Hard Aspects" perspective: The rationalization of public facilities has not been implemented (according to plan). The introduction of private sector vitality into the development, maintenance, management, and operation of public facilities is not progressing, and has not become a proper beneficiary burden of public facilities. The utilization of public assets has not progressed.

4. "Finance & Other Soft Aspects" perspective: Staff do not understand their local government's financial indicators. Financial analysis using public accounting has not been carried out. Public accounting is not utilized. A review of revenue (fees, service charges, reductions, etc.) and expenditure (subsidies, burden money, commissions, etc.) has not been conducted. Measures to increase revenue are not promoted.

5. "Public-Citizen Collaboration & Citizen Cooperation" perspective: Guidelines for public-citizen collaboration and citizen cooperation have not been established. The potential for public-citizen collaboration and citizen cooperation, whether hard or soft, remains unexamined. Private vitality through the designated administrator or other systems is not properly introduced, and outsourcing of counter services has not progressed, nor has the introduction of AI/RPA.

6. "Effectiveness & Improvement" perspective: A mechanism to improve the issues pointed out in the reform process has not been established. The results of reform are not reflected in the next comprehensive plan, the next year's budget, or personnel matters. Support for regional improvements is not provided.

And there are numerous others, for example, misunderstanding that the Designated Administrator System and PFI are inexpensive tools; failure to check the recipients of subsidies; misconception that one cannot intervene with designated administrators or autonomous associations; and thinking that projects mandated by the government or prefecture must be undertaken.

Taking into consideration the aforementioned challenges, I wish to propose seven guiding principles for the effective execution of reforms:

1. Reform initiatives should be anchored on sound, objective, equitable, and impartial criteria, and not on fleeting emotions. It is paramount that administrative evaluations are entrusted to competent and apt evaluators.

2. It is vital to maintain transparency throughout deliberative processes.

3. It is imperative to ensure that the intent behind reform (or its evaluation) transcends mere symbolic gestures and brings about substantive change.

4. It is advisable to adopt straightforward formats to alleviate undue strain on both the departments responsible for overseeing the reform (the evaluators) and the departments being assessed (the evaluatees).

5. Emphasis should be placed on optimizing role allocation to enhance efficiency and effectiveness.

6. Addressing jurisdictional concerns within the administration is essential, but an equally pivotal aspect is the cultivation of a synergistic relationship between public administrators and citizens. This entails fostering both collaborative public-citizen partnerships and active citizen participation.

7. Reform strategies should encompass regional nuances and variations, and the provision of intermediary support, where needed, is of paramount importance.

Procedures for Administrative Reform

Now, I shall discuss the procedures for administrative reform, with the process described as follows: ① Formulation of Comprehensive Plans (Reform Guidelines, Internal Control Policies) → ② Current Status Analysis ((i) Financial Analysis, (ii) Inventory of Business Operations (Workload Survey)) → ③ Review of Administrative Operations (Re-evaluation of Revenue & Expenditure, Etc.) → ④ Specific Improvements (Revision of Existing Systems, Introduction of Private Sector Vitality, Etc.) → ⑤ Regular Monitoring (Policy

Evaluation & Auditing).

The details of each step (phase) are described below.
1. Formulation of Comprehensive Plans (Reform Guidelines, Internal Control Policies)
Administrative management reform starts with the formulation of a comprehensive plan. All policies should be aligned with the comprehensive plan with no deviation. Since policy evaluation monitors the progress of reform, we can consider administrative management reform to originate with the formulation of the comprehensive plan. Within the overall comprehensive plan, the guidelines for administrative management reform are specifically outlined in the Reform Guidelines. From fiscal 2020, prefectures and government-designated cities have been obligated to establish internal control policies. Some local governments believe internal control is unrelated to administrative management reform, but its objectives, namely, ① Efficiency & Effectiveness of Business Operations, ② Reliability of Financial Reporting, ③ Compliance with Laws and Regulations, and ④ Preservation of Assets, are not new concepts and are consistent with those of previous administrative management reform and auditing. Municipalities implementing proper administrative management reform will likely have no issues with internal control or auditing, while those neglecting reform may encounter problems. Therefore, the formulation of a comprehensive plan (reform guidelines and internal control policies) is not merely a formality, but should be grounded in specific administrative management reform.

2. Current Status Analysis ((i) Financial Analysis, (ii) Inventory of Business Operations (Workload Survey))
Based on the guidelines mentioned above, the first task to be carried out in implementing specific administrative management reform is a current status analysis consisting of two main pillars. The first pillar is financial analysis. I recommend a financial analysis through local government accounting. Although all local governments disclose indicators under the Fiscal Health Law, along with the four financial statements of local government accounting (namely, ① balance sheet, ② profit and loss statement, ③ net asset change statement, and ④ cash flow statement), the actual financial situation is not fully revealed by these indicators based on single-entry accounting. For example, a Ministry of Internal Affairs and Communications' survey showed no entities with a real deficit amount (real deficit ratio over 0%) in fiscal 2016, but the Local Government Accounting Research Center calculated the annual differences for 1,549 local governments based on public accounting (double-entry accounting), revealing that 60 percent were in the red. Furthermore, merely preparing the four financial statements using public accounting is insufficient. For example, revealing only the administrative cost does not indicate whether it is high, low, or reasonable. Com-

parative analyses with similar entities, cost per resident, and other factors are necessary for evaluation. A combination of various indicators and comparisons with other local governments will reveal the financial situation of a municipality. Additionally, this financial analysis will clarify where costs are incurred in which departments as well as subsidies. Instead of blindly implementing administrative management reform, it is vital to first identify the issues specific to the municipality, and then revise the subsidies and the like accordingly.

3. Review of Administrative Operations

Based on the results of the financial analysis and inventory of operations, a specific review of administrative operations is undertaken. At this stage, unnecessary, historically completed, or low-priority projects are eliminated, while similar or overlapping operations are integrated or their jurisdiction altered (from government to private sector), or even expanded or newly established. Attention to detail is essential in the review of administrative operations. For instance, one cannot judge the overall quality of the Social Welfare Council Grant without carefully examining the individual components, such as "○○ Salon Activities" or "○○ Watch Activities," or breaking the grant down into specific areas, such as "District A, District B..." It is impossible to evaluate its appropriateness without doing so. I refer to this process as the "Segmented Grant Review." Furthermore, the review should classify expenditures such as subsidies, entrusted expenses, and burden funds, or revenues like usage fees or handling charges, and examine them separately. If a full review cannot be conducted, implementing it annually with designated themes is also a valid approach.

4. Specific Improvements

Once the above tasks are complete, concrete revisions to the existing systems and the introduction of private-sector vitality should be examined. For subsidies, entrusted expenses, and burden funds, guidelines can be abolished or revised. Usage fees and handling charges can also be amended or relief measures offered. In terms of business improvements, automation with RPA or digitization is a step to consider. Also, outsourcing to the private sector or adopting PFI or the Designated Administrator System for public facilities should be considered at this stage. Outsourcing can be introduced after clarifying the division of roles among regular staff, fiscal-year-based staff, and private enterprises based on an inventory of operations. Although different departments in municipalities may manage public facilities separately, this point should be considered in the context of overall administrative management. Careful scrutiny is required to avoid incorrect interpretations or improper operation, such as assuming that introducing private-sector vitality will reduce costs, or employing the Designated Administrator System where contracting would be more appropriate.

5. Regular Monitoring (Administrative Evaluation & Audit)

Finally, there is regular monitoring (administrative evaluation and audit). Administrative reform is not a one-time event, as continuous, regular evaluation and monitoring of policies (measures, administrative operations, etc.) are essential. Auditing is an important last resort since there is no legal compulsion in reform, but auditors have the right to rectify or recommend. Highly inappropriate uses of grants need to be pointed out by auditors. However, since the extensive tasks described above cannot be handled solely by a limited number of auditors, outsourcing auditing tasks is also possible, namely, external audits. This step is suitable for targeting specific themes or organizations. Even in policy evaluation, in addition to internal evaluations by administrative staff, third-party external evaluations should be conducted. While internal evaluation is mandatory, sole reliance can lead to it becoming a mere formality and create such problems as the inability to rigorously evaluate policies with vested interests. I believe it is desirable to establish a system of objective and rational evaluations conducted by neutral external experts.

References

※Masami Hiraishi, "Administrative Reform and the Logic and Development of NPM" in "Japan's Public Administration - A New Administration" (Hokju Publishing, 2014)
※Local Government Accounting Research Center, Analysis of Local Finances from the Perspective of Local Government Accounting" (2020)

Chapter 3

Comprehensive Plan and Administrative Evaluation

Shiga University, Koji Yokoyama

Introduction

As mentioned in Chapter 2, administrative reform starts with the formulation of a comprehensive plan. However, many local governments lack this awareness. As will be detailed later, a survey by the Ministry of Internal Affairs and Communications revealed that many local governments have not linked their comprehensive plans with administrative evaluations.

Administrative evaluation is the process of confirming the progress of policies stated in the comprehensive plan. Fundamentally, the formulation of a comprehensive plan involves taking stock of previous policies (measures and administrative tasks), evaluating and verifying them, scrapping those that have achieved their objectives, and planning new necessary measures and administrative tasks. This work should be the very essence of reform, but in reality, examples abound where policies (measures and administrative tasks) are merely submitted by various departments, compiled, and left at that. As superficial comprehensive plans, they often end up untouched, gathering dust without follow-up until the next formulation. There is no point in formulating a comprehensive plan in such a manner. A comprehensive plan is a fundamental policy for local government management, and is of utmost importance. In this chapter I would like to discuss what a comprehensive plan is and how administrative evaluation serves as a means of assessing and verifying the plan.

Development of the Comprehensive Plan

The comprehensive plan began with the 1969 amendment to the Local Autonomy Act, stipulated in Article 2, Section 4: "Cities, towns, and villages must establish a basic concept for comprehensive and planned administration in their region through the council's resolution, and act accordingly." Since then, it has become standard for most local governments to formulate a comprehensive plan. However, as the careful reader will have noticed, the mandate here is "basic concept," and there is no mention of a "basic plan" or "implementation plan." Also, this applies only to cities, towns, and villages, not to prefectures. Today, however, it has become natural even for prefectures to formulate comprehensive plans, and most local governments treat the basic concept and the basic plan as a set in the comprehensive plan.

However, in response to the growing trend of decentralization, the Local Autonomy Act was later partially amended (Act No. 35 of 2011) and promulgated on May 2, 2011, and enforced on August 1, 2011, with Article 2, Section 4 deleted.

Even without a legal obligation, comprehensive plans continue to be formulated by almost all local governments. Additionally, a notice from the Minister of Internal Affairs and Communications on the same day as the law's promulgation (General Affairs No. 57, City No. 51, May 2, 2011) stated, "It is still possible for individual cities, towns, and villages to continue to formulate their current basic concepts through the council's resolution based on the provisions of Article 96, Paragraph 2." As a result, few local governments today have established "basic ordinances for local autonomy" or "ordinances concerning matters to be resolved by the assembly" as the basis for formulating comprehensive plans or for assembly resolutions. The details of these circumstances will be discussed later.

What Is the Comprehensive Plan, and Its Significance

Now, let's discuss the comprehensive plan developed by local governments as outlined above. What exactly is a comprehensive plan?

The official website of Koriyama City in Fukushima Prefecture outlines the following: "A comprehensive plan is the highest-level plan in local government administration. It represents the future goals and measures of the municipality shared by all residents, providing a fundamental guideline for all residents, businesses, and administrations to act upon. To clarify the purposes and means of administrative management, the comprehensive plan is usually composed of three layers: basic concept, basic plan, and implementation plan, with each layer assuming the following roles:
Basic concept: Expresses the future goals and basic measures to achieve them.
Basic plan: Systematically outlines the content of the basic measures in each department based on the basic concept.
Implementation plan: Presents specific projects required for the planned implementation of the measures defined in the basic plan."

This description succinctly captures the essence of the comprehensive plan, but I would like to explore it in more detail.

I believe there are three aspects (significance) to the comprehensive plan:
1) Planning as the highest level of administration
2) Management strategy of the municipality as a business entity
3) Guideline for community development including residents

The first aspect, planning as the highest level of administration, holds the topmost position among the countless administrative plans across various policy fields, representing the basic concept of community-building, so to speak. Without this foundational thinking, each administrative department would proceed in disparate directions, unable to implement orderly, efficient, and effective policies.

In reality, having been involved in administrative reform and citizen collaboration policies in many municipalities, I often find myself exasperated by administrative silos. Even though areas like reform and collaboration are obligatory for all departments, it is not uncommon to find departments pretending that these matters do not concern them. This is evidence that the fundamental concepts of reform and collaboration are not shared within the municipality. Regardless of the field, all policies must be implemented efficiently and effectively, and it is essential to constantly check for collaboration and redundancy, and whether information is shared within the office. The basis for this should be the comprehensive plan. Unfortunately, few municipalities seem to practice this on a daily basis; otherwise, their comprehensive plans would not be gathering dust.

That is why, at least during the formulation of the comprehensive plan every few years, I would like to see efforts made to organize thoughts across the entire administration, identify each policy, and perform a scrap-and-build of measures and administrative businesses. During this time, I would also encourage a review and integration of the various administrative plans, as referred to in the Basic Policy on Economic and Fiscal Management and Reform decided by the Cabinet in June 2022, under Chapter 4: Medium to Long-Term Economic and Fiscal Management, 4. New Division of Roles between the Nation and Localities.

This does not mean that necessary plans or policies should be weakened or deemed unnecessary; it means integrating the plans or policies that can be more effective. Integrating an overall collaboration plan or reform guidelines into the comprehensive plan may be one example.

Along with this, it is worthwhile to consider the integration or abolition of accompanying councils and committees. The number of members should be kept to a skilled few. Committees filled only with the organization's staff strictly for show are meaningless.

Viewed from another angle, the comprehensive plan must also be a logic tree. A logic tree refers to a technique that unfolds relationships between events in a tree-like form through logic. It involves digging into the causes of results, or specifying the means to realize a certain goal.

In the context of the comprehensive plan, first there is a basic concept (e.g., creating a town where everyone can live with peace of mind), followed by policies to realize that concept (enhancing disaster prevention and security), with measures to realize the policy (promoting crime prevention activities) leading to administrative projects (subsidizing the installation of security cameras).

Is your municipality's comprehensive plan structured like a logic tree? Are policies devised logically? I have observed instances where basic concepts become mere catchphrases, or measures are just a collection of administrative projects, but this is putting the cart before the horse. Policies must be logical. I will elaborate on how to devise policies in a later chapter, but first, I would like you to reconsider whether your comprehensive plan is structured as a logic tree.

As for the second aspect, management strategy for municipalities as management entities, with the concept of NPM (New Public Management) now widespread, there is no shortage of efforts to introduce private-sector principles into administrations, for example, moving "from administration to management," embracing "customer-first principles," or applying comprehensive plan and administrative evaluation to management theories like the PDCA cycle (Plan→Do→Check→Action). However, since profit-seeking businesses and administrations promoting residents' welfare unmotivated by profit are fundamentally different, it is not about which is right or wrong. It may be unreasonable to consider all administrative activities based on corporate principles, but municipalities are also organizations, and as long as there are people and budgets involved, management is necessary. In that regard, the comprehensive plan holds meaning not just as an "administrative plan" but also as a "management strategy." It is not merely about gathering policies, but also about how to efficiently and effectively manage limited personnel and budgets for implementing those policies. Proper allocation of human resources, organizational restructuring, and budget distribution go beyond the mere administrative handling of personnel and fiscal evaluations. Viewing a municipality as a management entity and implementing strategic management are vital. The comprehensive plan is a guideline for medium to long-term management strategies.

The third aspect, guideline for community development including residents, means that managing a municipality, or "community development," cannot be achieved by an administration alone. No matter how many policies the administrative side may propose, they cannot be implemented without the cooperation of residents. As stated in Chapter 1, future public policies cannot be handled solely by an administration. Collaboration between administrations and the public is becoming indispensable in every policy field, and opportunities for residents to take the lead are increasing. In such times, if the direction in which the community is developing is unclear, then the residents will be at a loss. If the administration and citizens are looking in entirely different directions, community development will not progress. Therefore, it is necessary to formulate a comprehensive plan, not just as a guideline for the administration but also including the "policy of the town" and its residents. As will be explained later, there are examples of noting the division of roles between "public and private" in a comprehensive plan's policies, or defining "regional plans" for different areas. These can be said to strongly emphasize the aspect of the comprehensive plan as a guideline for community development including residents.

Formulation Status of the Comprehensive Plan

As for the formulation status of the comprehensive plan, no recent surveys have been conducted by the national government, so we refer to the Survey on the Actual Situation of Comprehensive Plans in Basic Municipalities published by the Japan Productivity Center, a public interest incorporated foundation, in September of Heisei 28 (2016). The questionnaire survey was conducted as of the end of February of Heisei 28, targeting 813 cities and wards and 745 towns across the country, with a response rate of 60.3 percent. Villages were not included in the target.

In the survey, 98.3 percent of the entities responded they had a "comprehensive plan during the planning period," while 1.7 percent responded they did not. Furthermore, 91.1 percent of the entities answered they "plan to formulate in the future," while a combined total of 8.5 percent responded "will not formulate" or "do not know." From this it can be understood that even though the legal obligation has been eliminated, most basic municipalities are currently formulating comprehensive plans and will continue doing so in the future.

Also, as the basis for formulating comprehensive plans, 18 percent of the entities are based on "autonomy basic ordinances," 12.8 percent on "comprehensive plan ordinances," 34.1 percent on "ordinances defining issues that should be resolved," and 6.4 percent on "other ordinances." Just over 20 percent (22.3%) of the entities answered they have "no basis," suggesting that formulating a comprehensive plan is perceived as a matter of course in most municipalities, regardless whether there is a legal basis or not.

The formulation status is described above. In this survey we are looking into such matters as the presence or absence of the so-called three-layered structure of "basic concept, basic plan, implementation plan, and district-specific plan" as well as the presence or absence of qualitative or numerical targets, the presence or absence of role distribution among various entities, and the relationship with the budget. I would like to introduce these items in the next section, incorporating my views as well.

Frequently Asked Questions

Next, I would like to answer some common questions often asked about the development of comprehensive plans, along with my views on them.

1. Q: Is a comprehensive plan necessary? → A: As previously mentioned, it is, of course, necessary to create such a plan.

2. Q: What is the appropriate planning period? → A: A 5- to 10-year timeframe is common, but in our rapidly changing modern society, continuous revision is essential. Even with a 5- to 10-year planning period, annual evaluations and verification may lead to necessary changes. Some municipalities align this with mayoral terms. According to a survey by the Japan Productivity Center on the Relationship between the Comprehensive Plan and the Terms of Mayors, 7.4 percent of the organizations replied that "the terms coincide." I do not think this approach is wrong, but because there are so many administrative matters that must continue irrespective of politics, they should not be influenced by the preferences of mayors.

3. Q: Is there a lack of connection with the organization, personnel, and finance? → A: In a survey by the Japan Productivity Center on whether the "comprehensive plan includes the budget," 40.4 percent answered "included," and 58.0 percent answered "not included." Nearly 60 percent of the municipalities do not link the budget. Furthermore, about the "relationship between the comprehensive plan's structure and the organization, departments, and sections," a total of 60.9 percent answered "completely matches" or "mostly matches." Conversely, a combined 35.8 percent answered "mostly does not match" or "have not specifically considered the relationship," suggesting that many municipalities do not reflect the comprehensive plan in their organization and personnel. A system reflecting personnel and finances proportionate to the comprehensive plan is necessary, or else the plan will remain a mere slogan.

4. Q: Should numerical targets be included? → A: Numerical targets are not always necessary, but the criteria for success must be clearly defined. In a survey by the Japan Productivity Center on whether "qualitative objectives are set," 90.8 percent of the organizations responded "set." In addition, 75.9 percent answered "set" for "are numerical targets set?" From my experience, most policies and administrative projects can set numerical targets, although many are improperly done. I will elaborate on this point later.

5. Q: Should the roles and responsibilities of each entity (public and private) be included? → A: As mentioned in Chapter 1, public policies should be supported by the division of roles between public and private entities. Therefore, the roles and responsibilities of each entity should be described as much as possible. A survey by the Japan Productivity Center found that 35.3 percent of organizations had this set, indicating a future increase.

6. Q: Should plans be made for each region? →A: To my recollection, many municipalities developed regional plans after the municipal mergers in the Heisei era, mostly as a mitigation measure. However, in recent years, few organizations seem to be formulating regional plans. In the earlier survey by the Japan Productivity Center, only 8.8 percent were developing district-specific plans. But with the nation's declining population, more detailed community policies may necessitate district-specific plans. It would be desirable to redefine these districts beyond traditional units.

7. Q: Is there a link between comprehensive plan and administrative evaluation. →A: In the same survey, regarding "whether the comprehensive plan is being evaluated," although 61.6 percent of the organizations responded "being evaluated," 36.7 percent responded "not being evaluated." As I have repeatedly mentioned, administrative evaluation is simply the evaluation and verification of the policies summarized in the comprehensive plan. The fact that the two are not linked is a typical bad example of both becoming mere formalities.

Many municipalities often seek advice on how to evaluate their administration and how to set performance indicators. In the next section, I will explain administrative evaluation.

Development of Administrative Evaluation

In Japan, the commencement of administrative evaluations is said to have begun with the Business and Project Evaluation System in Mie Prefecture in 1996. The fact that it began at the local level before the national government is particularly noteworthy.

Subsequently, the so-called Government Policy Evaluation Act, or the Act Concerning the Evaluation of Policies by Administrative Organs, was enforced from 2002, leading to the start of the policy evaluation system at the national level, which continues to this day. However, local governments are excluded from this system.

Given the spirit of local decentralization, it is only natural for local governments to conceive and execute administrative evaluations themselves. Unfortunately, due to the lack of legal obligation in some local governments, administrative evaluations are not being carried out, reflecting a disparity similar to the overall reform efforts. Moreover, even among municipalities that are conducting evaluations, methods vary and some problematic approaches have been observed.

In this paper I would like to introduce various aspects of the administrative evaluation, ranging from what it is to the setting of performance indicators.

What is Administrative Evaluation?

First, the term administrative evaluation can be defined collectively as "policy evaluation," "measure evaluation," and "business and project evaluation" in proportion to the policy system of the comprehensive plan. The terminologies used vary depending on the level of evaluation carried out by each local government.

Additionally, administrative evaluations can be classified in various ways, with three representative types listed below.

1. By timing: "preliminary evaluation," "interim evaluation," and "post-evaluation." Post-evaluation" is the most common among local governments.

2. By evaluator: "internal evaluation" and "external evaluation." Internal evaluation is mandatory and conducted by staff. External evaluation is performed by external experts, but not many municipalities implement it. I believe external evaluations should be mandatory, because relying only on internal evaluations may lead to bias. However, the selection of capable evaluators is crucial when introducing an external evaluation.

3. By whether measured numerically or not: "qualitative evaluation" and "quantitative evaluation. Quantitative evaluations have spread significantly among local governments,

but many feel challenged by how the indicators are set.

Status of the Introduction of Administrative Evaluations

Regarding the status of introducing administrative evaluations, let's refer to the Ministry of Internal Affairs and Communications' Survey Results on Administrative Evaluation Efforts in Local Public Entities published in June 2017.

In prefectures, designated cities, and municipalities, the percentage of entities that answered "already introduced" was 61.4 percent, but among "towns and villages" the figure was 38.9 percent, showing that smaller municipalities have not progressed in implementing administrative evaluations.

Moreover, 12.2 percent of the entities that "had implemented but later abolished" the administrative evaluation suggests a lack of proper knowledge, complexities in procedures, or increased staff burden.

The situation regarding the introduction of external evaluations shows that 46.5 percent of entities are conducting both internal and external evaluations, revealing a gradual increase in the number implementing external evaluations.

Furthermore, 87.3 percent of entities answered "Yes" to the introduction of "evaluation indicators (quantitative evaluation indicators)," indicating that many local governments are advancing in this area.

On the other hand, other survey items on "challenges in administrative evaluation" revealed that setting evaluation indicators stood out at 78.5 percent, with many local governments struggling with administrative evaluation tasks or indicator setting methods. I will explain the approach to setting evaluation indicators later on.

What reassured me in this survey was the relatively high percentage of reform-related results, such as "measures or projects were examined from the viewpoint of results" (78.3%) and "termination of business projects or budget reductions were connected" (53.9%). However, on the other hand, "utilization in budget compilation, etc." at 71.3 percent seems to indicate that the actual effectiveness of administrative evaluation, namely its reflection in the budget, remains weak.

What Are Evaluation Indicators?

If asked what evaluation indicators are, I would simply answer that they indicate "how much of our work has been accomplished." Many municipal officials, confused by difficult expert talk and excessive textbook reading, struggle with this concept. After reading my explanation, I believe you will understand that evaluation indicators are not difficult.

In terms of textbooks, evaluation indicators consist of input indicators → output indicators (activity indicators) → outcome indicators (performance indicators).

To explain further, input indicators refer to the amount invested to carry out administrative activities. For example, this might include budget amounts, project costs, number of personnel involved, and total working hours. Next, output indicators refer to the amount of administrative activity carried out by inputting those resources. Examples include the distance of road maintenance or the number of lifelong learning lectures held. Finally, outcome indicators are about the achievements resulting from administrative activities. For instance, in road maintenance it could be a reduction in traffic congestion, or in lifelong learning the proficiency level of the learners.

Various policies are implemented with the ultimate outcome in mind, thereby making the outcome indicator the final goal. However, in cases where it is difficult to set an outcome indicator, some municipalities use the "output" indicator as an administrative evaluation measure. The problem created is that many municipalities completely confuse the two indicators, with administrative evaluation becoming unclear. In the following section I will explain the results of the review of administrative evaluation indicators I conducted in a particular municipality, categorizing the problems and prescribing solutions.

Examples of Common Mistakes in Evaluation Indicators

There are three commonly observed mistakes in evaluation indicators.

1. Confusing Output with Outcome: The resolution of a task is the outcome, while the number of meetings held to resolve the task is the output. The target is not how many meetings are held, but to what degree the issue is resolved.

2. Unclear Accumulation Basis: This can be roughly divided into three patterns:

① Cases where the "denominator" (target number) is not clear. For instance, if a goal is set for "500 participants," it makes sense if there are 1,000 targets (achieving 50%), but just stating 500 is ambiguous.

② Cases where the goal (end point) is not clear. For example, when stating "developing 10 km² of area," if the overall plan is to develop 100km², it means the aim for the year is to complete 10 percent. Without a clear final goal, the significance of the 10km² cannot be understood.

③ Cases requiring verification of whether the standards align with national or prefectural standards, or other similar entities. For example, even if a town aims for a certain percentage, the target needs to be verified against national or prefectural standards or compared with similar organizations.

As a reference, Kyoto City Hall has established a guideline called the Objective Indicator Setting Manual, which explains specific ways to set target values. Specifically, it introduces four methods of setting target values:

① Goals based on existing plans, e.g., the Disaster Prevention Plan targeting the development of fire-resistant water tanks and wells.

② Goals based on trends, e.g., the annual number of meals delivered through catering services.

③ Goals set considering financial situations and citizen needs, e.g., the consumer consultation resolution rate (%).

④ Goals considering external factors, e.g., the number of elderly club members.

Regardless, the emphasis is not simply on presenting numbers, but on setting values grounded in a solid rationale.

3. Inappropriate Units: For instance, whether it is appropriate to represent something in numbers, participants, rate (percentage), or progress (achievement). The best unit representing the task should be utilized. For instance, if you say "conduct an inspection once," it might be more informative to say "inspect 30 locations" if 30 sites are checked in that one instance. Similarly, "holding a lecture once" can give a different impression if presented as "one lecture = 50 participants."

Additionally, two questions frequently asked are (1) Is it necessary to set evaluation indicators for routine work? The answer is yes. As mentioned earlier, the objective of administrative evaluations is to depict the reality. Even for routine tasks, it is vital to communicate the volume of work and its efficiency; and (2) Is it acceptable not to establish precise numerical targets? Evaluation indicators are not solely for external display. Their primary purpose is to depict the reality. For example, it is misleading to report increasing figures when group membership is clearly declining. Certain projects may have potential that is only achievable with sufficient funding. In these instances, transparency about what is attainable within the available budget is vital.

In conclusion, administrative evaluations have two main objectives. The first is to introspectively assess the progress of our tasks, which is generally recognized. The second objective is to communicate to external stakeholders the scope and quality of our work. For instance, if a single inspection encompasses multiple sites, it is crucial to relay this information to the external parties. Indicators should therefore accurately reflect the reality as much as possible.

Administrative evaluations are not merely about establishing metrics. Through continual assessment using these numbers, the significance of each project becomes clear. Inefficient approaches should be revisited, and projects no longer holding relevance or offering a low cost-benefit ratio ought to be discontinued. Administrative evaluations are designed to steer these enhancements.

References

※Public Interest Incorporated Foundation Japan Productivity Center, "Survey on the Reality of Comprehensive Plans of Basic Local Governments," Survey Results Report (September 2016)
※Koriyama City official website, "What is the Comprehensive Plan?" https://www.city.koriyama.lg.jp/soshiki/21/5842.html (referenced in December 2022)
※Cabinet Office, "Basic Policies for Economic and Fiscal Management and Reform" (June 2022)
※Ministry of Internal Affairs and Communications, "Survey Results on the Status of Administrative Evaluations in Local Public Bodies" (June 2017)
※Katsuhiro Inazawa, "Introduction and Utilization of Administrative Evaluations" (Imagine Publishing, 2012)
※Hiraki Tanaka, "Strategic Evaluation of Local Governments" (Toyo Keizai Shinposha, 2014)
※Kyoto City General Planning Bureau, "Guidance on Indicators for Policy Evaluation" (2014)

Chapter 4

Policy Formulation and Administrative Work Review

Shiga University, Koji Yokoyama

Introduction

In the previous chapter I discussed the relationship between the comprehensive plan and the administrative evaluation. Essentially, comprehensive planning combines policies, strategies, and administrative projects from each department, making it important to formulate good policies. However, surprisingly, in local government settings, policies are often formulated without firmly understanding the concept of policy formulation.

In this chapter I would like to delve into the mindset behind policy formulation. At the same time, it is no exaggeration to say that these concepts shape the perspective from which we review administrative projects. Reviewing administrative projects simply means returning to each project's starting point, and rethinking why the policy was created and whether its methods are appropriate.

What is Policy?

First, let's look at the nature of policy, or public policy. Tatsuya Ono defines public policy as "a set of activities to realize the purpose and goals of responding to regional issues with public character, combining various resources to execute them, and including the process of affecting the region from the planning stage to implementation." Furthermore, Yukio Adachi views public policy as "a policy or action strategy to address public issues distinguished from purely private matters and those unique to specific groups, and among public policies, those formally adopted and implemented by the government are referred to as 'government policies.'"

In simple terms, I think a policy is a "prescription for solving regional public problems." For example, there are "problems that need to be solved" in the region, problems that cannot be left unattended, and there should be an "ideal image (region)" after the problems are solved. Between the current state and issues of the region and the ideal image (region) are various barriers, hurdles, and bottlenecks. The strategy of removing them gradually and filling in the gaps is what I consider "policy." To give an easy example, let's say a region suffers from many traffic accidents. This is a regional issue. In this case, the goal is a region with zero traffic accidents. Installing guardrails, improving roads, or setting up speed traps and automatic control systems are specific policies (strategies and administrative projects).

Elements of Policy

Now, let's look at the concept of policy formulation. When formulating a policy, it is essential to clarify the "policy elements," "financial elements," and "policy decision-making process." In this section, I want to discuss the policy elements for which I think there are seven main points.

The first point is "purpose." This perspective focuses on questions such as "Why is this measure being implemented?" "What do we want to solve?" and "What kind of society are we aiming for?" This purpose is the most important perspective in policy formulation. When I conduct administrative work reviews in local governments, I often find projects whose purpose is unknown. When asking government employees, I am sometimes told "because the previous mayor said to create it," but this is hardly a sufficient reason. That previous mayor must have had a reason, but if the purpose is now unclear, the project should be abandoned. And if a request from the current mayor or councilors does not align with the public interest and serves only the interests of some supporters, it does not constitute public policy.

The second point is "goal." This perspective includes questions like "Where is the target point?" "When should it be achieved?" and "How far must we go to call it a success?" This perspective, along with purpose, is often unclear and simply implementing policies without clear direction. No matter what the policy is, there must be a goal. Subsidies, in particular, should have an endpoint and be reviewed. Even routine tasks should set a specific end date and periodically verify whether they are being implemented efficiently and effectively, and whether the methods are appropriate. And this goal corresponds to the outcome indicators mentioned in the previous chapter on administrative evaluation. Without a goal, administrative evaluation indicators cannot be set.

The third point is "market." This perspective considers questions such as "What are the regional challenges (needs)?" "What are the difficulties?" and "Is this an issue that should be addressed publicly?" As mentioned earlier, if policy is a prescription for solving regional public issues, then understanding the market becomes essential. Without a clear idea of the market, policy planning cannot proceed. Consider private companies: would they develop products without analyzing the market first? Companies failing to do so would soon go out of business, wouldn't they? However, in local governments, policies are often made without this analysis. First, it is important to understand that "market" = "current regional status and challenges (needs)."

The fourth point is "target." This perspective asks, "Who is the effort for?" "What is the targeted demographic?" and "Does it benefit specific individuals, regions, or organizations?" There are numerous cases where policies have been drafted without properly defining these aspects, just like the previously mentioned perspectives. For example, creating an ad-hoc subsidy system without defining the target audience, thinking that anyone raising their hand will suffice. Policies must always have a specific target. This becomes the denominator when setting administrative evaluation indicators. If the number of people to be targeted within the jurisdiction and the percentage to be subsidized are not set, the policy will fail, and evaluation and verification cannot be performed.

The fifth point is "how." This perspective questions "How is the problem solved?" "What are the specific measures and projects?" and "Is the method appropriate?" If policy is a prescription for solving regional public issues, "how" becomes part of each policy. Is the currently implemented or planned policy or measure a prescription that solves the problem? Just as administering the wrong medicine will not cure the disease, it is necessary to formulate policies that can solve the problems at hand. And this corresponds to the output indicators in administrative evaluation.

The sixth point is "position." This perspective looks into such questions as "What role does the administration (citizens, businesses) play?" and "What areas will the administration (citizens, businesses) cover?" As stated repeatedly, public policy cannot be handled by the administration alone. It is not a matter of abandoning its role, but strengthening the capabilities of citizens and regions, and supporting the areas to be handled collaboratively. Many subsidies and other systems exist for this purpose. Yet, many local governments create subsidies without overseeing the distribution of public-private roles. First, it is necessary to clarify which parts of the public policy are to be handled by the administration and citizens (region), which parts are to be carried out collaboratively, and then plan the policies.

Finally, there is "literacy." This perspective considers questions like "Is there sufficient literacy to implement the policy?" "Is the environment prepared for implementing the policy?" "Is the training adequate?" and "Is there ample introduction of private-sector vitality?" Even with the previous six points, a policy implemented without literacy will not succeed. Literacy includes the expertise and technical skills required to implement policy, including the use of information systems and other environmental preparations. Staff training and human resource development are necessary to equip these literacies, as are "RPA" and "DX promotion" in information systems. In areas requiring high expertise that cannot be handled by administrative officers alone, outsourcing and introducing private-sector vitality come into play. Also, if the future public policy assumes that it will be handled by public-private role-sharing, it will also be necessary to concurrently carry out human resource development and DX promotion for citizens and regional groups.

Elements of Finance

Policy and budget are inseparable elements, meaning that a policy without a corresponding budget is unthinkable. The notion among some municipalities that it is acceptable to have an administrative officer work gratis without a budget is absurd. Conversely, some local governments invest budgets liberally for events and facility construction based on their mayor's manifesto, an approach that should be rejected outright.

All policies must be devised with a close eye on value for the money. In other words, it is crucial to consider, "Is the budget allocated to a measure worth the cost?" and "Do the effects increase with that budget allocation?" Furthermore, it is essential to constantly examine the situation from both hard and soft aspects. For example, to properly analyze the cost-effectiveness of social education policies, one must look at both the cost of managing facilities and the cost of the programs being conducted there.

A common tendency among municipal employees is to dismiss citizen or community requests with "it can't be done because there's no money." However, few local governments have a surplus budget, and the financial management of a municipality lies in how well it can make do with limited resources. Naturally, restricted funds mean that priorities must be considered, and strategies like scrap-and-build initiatives and proper budget allocation must be employed to find the funds for new projects, and therefore reform is essential. In my view, when municipalities claim something cannot be done for the lack of funds, they are really saying, "We can't meet our citizens' needs because we haven't undertaken reform."

Clarification of the Policy Decision-Making Process

Another important point to consider in policy formulation is the "clarification of the policy decision-making process." This is a given for well-functioning municipalities, but it is crucial for all. A significant cause of dissatisfaction among residents is not merely that budgets are not allocated, but more often complaints like "Why is the demand from that region (group) considered while our region (group) is ignored?"

The initiation of policies typically comes from executive proposals, legislative proposals, and requests from residents/groups. These proposals are refined through deliberative councils and, after public explanation or public comment, are decided by the executive branch, with the mayor at the top. It does not end there, however; they are also considered by the assembly as proposals, and officially decided through assembly resolutions.

Residents often become frustrated when it is unclear who, where, and why a decision is made to allocate budgets to a particular region (group), especially when the demands of vocal regions (groups) are met without rational grounds or transparent scrutiny.

Such opaque policy decision-making processes may lead to scandals. In fact, it is no exaggeration to say that most scandals stem from this lack of transparency.

This applies not only to governmental offices but also to community groups. Hence, it is essential in public policy to make clear the rationale for policy formulation and the process of decision-making.

Revisiting Policy

To sum up this section, policy can be defined as a prescription to solve public issues in a region. The elements of policy formulation include seven components ranging from purpose to literacy. These are also points for reviewing policies.

Finance is an inseparable and essential element in policy formulation. Reasons for financial mobilization, calculation basis, priority, and cost-effectiveness must be clarified. Municipalities must not use the excuse of lacking funds. More often, the problem lies in budget distribution and the methods of expenditure.

Additionally, policy formulation must make clear the decision-making process. In other words, who decides when and where, and the responsibility must be transparent. Most scandals occur against the background of an opaque policy decision-making process.

Administrative officers must not forget the fundamentals of policy formulation and the decision-making process based on evidence, not only to protect themselves from undue pressure and scandals but also as a principle of their work.

Revisiting the System and Style of Administrative Operations

Lastly, I would like to discuss the ideal system and approach for reviewing subsidies and other financial matters. I will present examples of the management approaches and systems of administrative operation reviews that I have been involved in both inside and outside Shiga Prefecture in recent years. There are three main characteristics of administrative operations.

First, the review of administrative operations is conducted in private. Although we refer to the review as "private," the contents of the discussions, the judgment results, and reasons are disclosed at a later date. However, methods such as live broadcasting with observers present are not used because they do not reveal the true feelings of the staff. The administrative operation reviews that I conduct, which will be detailed further, involve a tripartite group of a third-party expert, financial reform division, and relevant administrative division. Rather than criticizing the original division, we jointly explore ways to eliminate unnecessary operations and consider whether there are more efficient methods. By doing this, constructive reviews of administrative operations can be conducted.

Second, regarding the evaluators, the plan is to gather experts in local government, law, accounting, labour, and other fields. It is acceptable within specific fields to include specialists in welfare and representatives of the residents. However, the essential point is to make judgments based on expertise. Decisions made by a group of amateurs can weaken arguments, especially when facing opposition from the assembly. Unbiased experts rationally assessing from legal, accounting, or labour perspectives make it difficult to argue against opinions that certain practices should be stopped. Conversely, this means that decisions must be made that leave no room for rebuttal.

Third, the review sheet for administrative operations should be simplified as much as possible by reusing budget request documents and linking them directly to the budget. These efforts can reduce the burden on the original division and ensure greater effectiveness when linked to the budget. For reforms to be meaningful, they must be connected to personnel matters and the budget. In this regard, adjusting the budget request sheet may be a good idea. Other options could include reusing general plan evaluation and other review sheets. Some local governments have practiced combining administrative work evaluation sheets, reform review sheets, and budget request sheets into a single sheet. Documents like the Report on Major Policy Outcomes for the assembly's final account review can also be combined. These actions will greatly reduce the burden on staff who previously had to write the same details every time and enable the integration of comprehensive planning, reform, and finance. In any case, the main principle is "simple is best."

The above-mentioned management and organizational structure can be adopted not only for reviewing administrative projects, but also for revisiting subsidies, contributions, and other phases of administrative management reform. I sincerely hope you will take these suggestions into consideration.

References

※Tatsuya Ono, "Introduction to Regional Policy–Regional Development for the Future" (Minerva Shobo, 2008)
※Yukio Adachi, "What is Public Policy Studies?" (Minerva Shobo, 2009)

Chapter 5

Financial Analysis Based on Local Government Accounting

(General Accounting & Public Enterprise Accounting)

Representative Director, County Consulting, Inc., Koji Hirose

Introduction

The history of local government accounting is relatively new, and while there are aspects still being developed, local government accounting has evolved as an essential tool for accurately grasping the fiscal state of local public entities. The creation and disclosure of the four financial statements, along with a basic financial analysis, have become the focus of financial departments. Unfortunately, it cannot be said that they are effectively utilized in administrative reform. Moreover, from its early stages, public enterprise accounting adopted corporate accounting methods. Regrettably, many entities depend entirely on deficit compensation from general accounting as they are unable to manage independently.

Therefore, it is essential to promote administrative reform by expanding the understanding not only of financial departments but also among the management-related departments regarding the real meaning, viewpoints, and methods of using local government accounting and public enterprise accounting.

In this chapter I want to explain the fundamental details of financial analysis through local government accounting, positioned as a "health report card" for implementing administrative management reform.

What Is Local Government Accounting?

Government accounting, being "accounting," involves recording, aggregating, calculating, and reporting economic transactions in monetary value. Accounting in general can be broadly divided into "for-profit accounting" and "non-profit accounting," with local government accounting belonging to the latter category.

Aggregated results are prepared in the form of financial statements, revealing to stakeholders the performance and financial conditions. An essential point here is that all these documents are created through double-entry bookkeeping. There are two methods of recording transactions: single-entry bookkeeping and double-entry bookkeeping. A simple example illustrates their difference. Suppose you pay 1,000 yen in cash for an electricity bill. In single-entry bookkeeping you only record "electricity charge 1,000 yen" in the cash ledger. In contrast, double-entry bookkeeping also creates an electricity charge account and records "paid 1,000 yen in cash." Thus, single-entry bookkeeping records only cash receipts and disbursements, while double-entry bookkeeping also records the reason for the cash flow, in this case being electricity charges. It goes without saying that double-entry book-keeping is advantageous for data analysis and management.

Explanation of Financial Documents in Local Government Accounting

Among the financial documents, the four financial statements consist of four sheets (balance sheet, profit and loss statement, net worth statement, and cash flow statement). Supplementary documents provide detailed information on the main items of the four financial statements. Notes describe the criteria for creating the four financial statements and act as a rulebook, with both documents serving as supplementary explanations. Also, the fixed asset ledger plays a vital role in public accounting as a comprehensive record of the entity's fixed assets from acquisition to disposal or sale. Fixed assets account for over 90 percent of the total assets held by local public bodies, so the quality of this ledger significantly affects the balance sheet figures and many stock-related plans. Reassessment is essential for future utilization, and the precision of the fixed asset ledger may impact policy decisions. Thus, we hope for careful management with high awareness. There have been cases where contractors cut corners and take on jobs at low cost, raising questions about the staff's project management ability. As an uneven maintenance measure depending on the contractor's level, it may be effective to set maintenance standards within the entity in advance.

Next, I will explain the four main financial statements. First, the balance sheet consists of assets, liabilities, and net assets, representing the organization's financial condition. You can confirm the aging progress of assets, the balance of assets and liabilities, and the amount of bad debts (delinquent claims) on this sheet. Second, the profit and loss statement aggregates the annual administrative cost by allocation (personnel costs, property costs, etc.), allowing the total annual cost and balance to be understood. However, it is necessary to add purpose-based elements (costs related to tourism, road maintenance, school lunches, etc.) for future utilization. The net worth statement documents the difference between assets and liabilities, or the surplus portion. You can judge profitability (whether administrative costs are covered by financial resources) on this sheet. The point is that the organization is not sustainable unless it is covered by financial resources, including not only cash expenditures but also non-cash costs such as depreciation expenses. Lastly, the cash flow statement displays cash receipts and payments in three categories (business activities, investment activities, and financial activities). You can verify what the money was used for and its type on this sheet. The ideal is business activities plus, investment activities minus, financial activities minus, and this year's cash flow positive, which means normal operations generating funds used for public investment, advancing local bond redemption, and still leaving a surplus.

Units of Preparation and Their Effects

Next, I will discuss the units of preparation for these financial documents. Three types of preparation are required: general accounting, overall accounting, and consolidated accounting. General accounting captures the core tendencies of the organization; overall accounting includes special accounting to grasp the overall tendencies; and consolidated accounting captures the trends of the organizational group, including partnerships, wide-area unions, and the third sector. The preparation of these financial documents sheds light on the status of assets and liabilities, the uneven distribution of administrative costs, and the surplus or deficit of financial resources within the organization.

This can be likened to a "physical measurement" that allows characteristics such as height, weight, chest circumference, and grip strength to be known. However, this is merely a physical measurement and not on the level of a "health examination." Care must be taken to recognize this point, as a health examination requires a more detailed analysis.

Historical Background and Necessity of Local Government Accounting

Let's take a look at the relatively short history of the local government accounting system. The New Local Government Accounting System Research Council Report was published in May 2006, initiating a significant trend. Two months later, in July, a practical study group was launched, and in June 2007, the Local Public Entity Fiscal Health Law was enacted. Four months later, in October, a working group was established to promote the development of local public accounting, evolving into a more concrete dimension. Various models such as the Ministry of Internal Affairs and Communications Model, Standard Model, Tokyo Metropolitan Model, and Osaka Prefecture Model were subsequently created. To address this proliferation, a uniform local public accounting manual was published in January 2015, leading us to the present. However, a significant event necessitating local public accounting occurred within this flow, that being the financial collapse of Yubari City. In 2007, Yubari City experienced a financial collapse, becoming a fiscal reconstruction organization unable to function as a local government entity. The closure of coal mines due to the energy revolution led to a rapid population decline and excessive debt burden. Attempts to transition to the tourism industry also failed, culminating in a situation involving the concealment of deficits and financial manipulation. The population, which was 116,908 at its peak, is predicted to fall below 3,000 by 2040. ※

These facts were late to come to light precisely because of the inadequacy of the city's accounting system. At the time of its financial crisis, Yubari City had financial statements showing income and expenses, as well as various statistical reports. However, it lacked a modern, comprehensive local public accounting system. This lack made a detailed and complete evaluation of the city's financial status through accounting measures challenging. It's crucial to recognize that financial statements and statistical data are essential for informed decision-making.

From these factors, local public accounting can be viewed as a type of health examination necessary to understand and improve public financial conditions; it is a tool for preventing bankruptcy (to keep life going) and for making accurate management decisions (for effective treatment).

Main Financial Analysis

The following section deals with financial analysis in local public accounting, but first I would like to briefly organize the concept of depreciation, the most important aspect in understanding local public accounting.

As shown in the principle of cost allocation in corporate accounting, depreciation refers to allocating the acquisition cost of an asset as an expense over the asset's useful lifespan. For example, if constructing a 100 million-yen building with a useful lifespan of 50 years, the cost is not recorded as 100 million yen in the year of construction, but is allocated over 50 years. Specifically, 100 million yen ÷ 50 years = 2 million yen is recorded as the "depreciation expense" in the administrative cost calculation statement for 50 years. By allocating the 100 million-yen cost over the years of the building's use, the cost calculation for each fiscal year becomes appropriate.

Let me also briefly explain the "self-financing effect" aspect of depreciation. Self-financing means generating funds on one's own. Considering the previous example, the administrative cost of 2 million yen in depreciation expense is recorded annually, but unlike other costs, there is no cash expenditure. Recall the net asset change statement. If the administrative cost is only the depreciation expense of 2 million yen, and the cash income is 2 million yen, the difference for the current fiscal year is zero. However, considering the actual cash balance, the cash income is 2 million yen and the cash expenditure is zero, resulting in a 2 million-yen surplus. Thus, depreciation expense has the effect of generating funds. While most municipalities currently face significant social issues due to insufficient funds for the renewal of infrastructure assets built in the past, if the amount equivalent to the depreciation expense were set aside in a fund every year, there would be no shortage of funds. But, if the amount is 2 billion yen, not 2 million, it becomes practically impossible. However, showing the direction to set aside at least 1 or 2 percent for essential assets, many municipalities have enacted ordinances for setting aside such funds.

① Per Capita Fixed Asset Value

The formula is given as "Fixed Asset Value / Population." The previously held view that a higher value indicates better services for residents and hence pursued for better urban planning is now seen as outdated. In an era marked by a declining population and escalating social welfare costs due to an aging society, it is imperative to maintain a compact asset base. Limited resources must be wisely allocated and maintenance costs closely controlled. The primary objective of this indicator is to gauge the appropriate scale of held assets. It is essential to use the acquisition price, not the book value, for fixed assets in this metric. Using book value may conflate the effects of depreciation, leading to incorrect assessments. Moreover, smaller municipalities, especially those with populations below 5,000, tend to have a higher ratio. The costs for public projects do not scale down linearly with the population. Hence, caution is needed when analyzing data for these municipalities.

② Per Capita Fund Balance

The formula is given as "Fund Balance / Population." Funds are essentially reserves, and having more is always beneficial. A main point is to ensure that funds for asset renewal are set aside. Systematic annual allocation, for instance, to a Public Facility Maintenance Fund, can facilitate this. Establishing such practices in by-laws might also be a prudent policy.

③ Per Capita Debt Amount

The formula is given as "Total Liabilities / Population." Debt consists of items like local bonds, provisions for retirement bonuses, and unpaid expenses. Local bonds are particularly noteworthy given their magnitude and long redemption periods. Local bonds must be repaid, often over durations as long as 50 years. While the current generation benefits from borrowed funds, it is the future generations that bear the repayment burden, making it desirable to limit expenditures that may constrain future generations. Continually borrowing to repay existing debt can trap municipalities in a vicious cycle. Some advocate for substantial borrowing with complex justifications, but the basic principle that excessive debt can lead to fiscal instability remains unchanged. This reality makes it vital to evaluate debt in the context of assets, and to consider special fiscal measures as important.

④ Net Asset Ratio

The formula is given as "Net Asset Value / Total Asset Value." A higher ratio is often associated with financial stability due to reduced obligations from local bonds. However, understanding why the ratio is high is essential; if due to depreciated assets, significant renewals might loom and pose fiscal challenges. Comprehensive financial analysis should combine multiple indicators. Infrastructure assets such as roads and bridges have limited liquidity. Thus, assessing financial stability might require evaluating the "real net asset ratio," which excludes such non-liquid assets. The ratio will likely be lower, especially when considering public enterprise accounts. Many municipalities even face a negative balance, exposing the financial vulnerabilities of public enterprises. Improving the financial health of public enterprises is clearly paramount, even more so than general accounting.

⑤ Tangible Fixed Asset Depreciation Rate

The formula is given as "Accumulated Depreciation Amount / Depreciable Asset Acquisition Value." The commonly known "obsolescence ratio" indicates the extent to which the value of assets, excluding land and non-depreciable assets, has depreciated since their acquisition or construction. As of fiscal 2018, the national average stood at approximately 60 percent. The author speculates an annual progression in obsolescence between 2 and 5 percent. It should be noted that 60 percent is merely an average; thus for individual assets such as administrative buildings, roads, school facilities, and bridges, it is crucial to manage their specific depreciation rates and prioritize asset renewal. Accurate individual asset data registered in the fixed asset ledger are also imperative. Unfortunately, there are firms that offer public accounting support at low costs and skimp on maintaining the fixed asset ledger, negligence that can hinder accurate decision-making for asset renewal and potentially jeopardize public safety. In one case the author encountered, a significant road renovation project from the previous year was not registered as an asset. Municipal staff often struggle to discern the quality of accounting support providers. Therefore, it is recommended that internal asset management standards be established, inconsistencies in fixed asset ledger management be prevented, and the fixed asset ledger be periodically reviewed.

⑥ Per Capita Net Administrative Cost

The formula is given as "Net Administrative Cost / Population." It is important to gauge the costs associated with administrative activities. While a lower value is preferable, a comparison with other entities can be useful. Each entity features unique circumstances affecting their administrative costs. A comparison across different entities can uncover unexpected facts, find other causative factors, or discover previously overlooked realities. Moreover, breaking down these costs (e.g., per capita subsidies, per capita personnel expenses) can offer additional insights. A key point to note is the inclusion of costs like depreciation, which does not involve cash outflow. Even with the current local public accounting system emphasizing cash outflow, allocating resources towards administrative costs, including depreciation, produces a surplus. This surplus, reflected in the change in net assets for the year, can be channeled into an asset renewal fund, underscoring the significance of the accrual-based system.

⑦ Beneficiary Burden Ratio

The formula is given as "Ordinary Revenue / Ordinary Administrative Cost." This ratio represents the proportion of administrative costs covered by fees and charges levied on residents, serving as an indicator of the self-sustainability of administrative activities. Rather than focusing only on the overall value, breaking it down by specific projects or facilities can make fee revisions more tangible. For instance, by investigating the costs associated with Facility A, one can assess whether its usage fee is too high, or too low, or just right, enabling evidence-based policy decisions.

Concerns of Fiscal Insolvency and Cost Rigidity

Up to this point, we have examined various indicators that bring us to a notable conclusion regarding entities with "fears of fiscal insolvency" and those experiencing "cost rigidity."

Entities with fears of fiscal insolvency are defined as those with a net asset ratio falling below the 35.5 percent of Yubari City, and concurrently possessing a real net asset ratio that is negative or nearly so. Omitting local government names, large cities in Kyushu and towns and villages in the Tohoku region can be cited as many struggle from unavoidable circumstances, such as increased restoration costs due to natural disasters. The worst entity has a net asset ratio of 31.0 percent and a real net asset ratio of -18.8 percent.

Entities experiencing cost rigidity refer to those where the per capita subsidy and per capita other account disbursements are more than twice the average value based on population size. Again, many towns and villages in Hokkaido, Kyushu, and Shikoku can be cited. Subsidies and other account disbursements are not costs that can be improved in the short term. Especially the latter necessitates financial reforms at the source, making certain expenditures unavoidable and limiting budget allocations to other policies. While instant improvements are unrealistic, a thorough review of subsidies and public enterprise reforms remains an urgent matter.

Profit and Loss Statement by Purpose

The four financial statements under public accounting showcase the consolidated figures of an entity. While systemically essential and useful, from a financial analysis perspective they resemble basic physical measurements. To ensure a comprehensive diagnosis and effective treatment of an ailment, detailed health check data are indispensable.

By conducting an administrative cost analysis based on "administrative purpose" and "character," one can pinpoint where and what (for instance, tourism expenses are excessively subsidized) and further delve into the more intricate "cost analysis by administrative service." Future project reviews should undoubtedly be rooted in actual quantitative evidence.

Public Enterprises

The history of the Local Public Enterprise Act is long, and corporate accounting methods were introduced early on for waterworks, hospital management, and the like. As such, the history of financial analysis for management started earlier than public accounting. Various financial analysis indicators have been published and are analyzed for their management status. But frankly, it is questionable whether these analytical results are actually utilized to improve public enterprise management. Care must be taken when using the depreciation rate prior to the legal application since the tangible fixed asset depreciation rate resets the depreciation expense at the time of legal application. We must evaluate these financial indicators comprehensively and strive for structural improvements in the financial framework. Deficits cannot be covered from general accounting indefinitely.

Sections Requiring Business Management Skills

Since public enterprises assume an independent accounting system, sustainable management responsibility arises therein. Transfers from general accounting are limited to standard internal transfers, and efforts must be made to pursue profit while satisfying the fairness and public nature of residential services. I believe this field requires exacting personnel with the sensibility to understand the contradictions and limits between public and private.

Hence, voices from the field should include such concerns as "What should be used for rate revision?" "It is difficult to understand being in-between private accounting and public accounting," "The system seems flexible but is actually restrictive," "Tax audits are worrisome due to a lack of expertise in consumption tax calculations," "There are no business initiatives due to the absence of technical experts," and "I don't understand the financial status or management goals to model." Resolving these issues requires proactive involvement of accountants, and building a solid management foundation is a challenge facing today's modern Japan.

Current Situation of Deficit Compensation

As previously mentioned, public enterprises are supposed to cover costs and expenses through fee revenue, invest in facilities, and record profits in their original form. However, the reality for many public enterprises is that large amounts of transfers are contributed from general accounting as deficit compensation.

Let's consider the case of a private company. Municipal water supply business accounting and sewage business accounting are equivalent to private company "subsidiaries." What happens if a subsidiary continues to incur annual deficits and receives massive capital injections from the parent company? First, the management's responsibility will be questioned at the shareholders' meetings, and financial institutions will review the lending conditions. Funds turned over to the subsidiary will not be acknowledged as losses for tax purpose, and a certain amount will be subject to taxation. Further, a massive restructuring plan for the subsidiary will be announced, possibly leading to closure or business transfers, with all these decisions and determinations happening swiftly.

This does not happen with local public bodies, but I think the situation is basically the same. A strong sense of crisis and tension, along with conscious reform as managers handling public funds, is required.

Therefore, I would like to propose the following seven items for public enterprise reform

1. Prioritize improvement over general accounting

2. Thoroughly recognize the independent accounting system

3. Stop making non-standard transfers to pretend to be profitable

4. Recognize there is no surplus in general accounting

5. Determine fees based on the results of cost calculations

6. Establish a reform committee with administrative reform departments and financial departments.

7. Review business strategies annually.

Conclusion

So, what do you think about the explanation of financial analysis through local public accounting? Like humans, both enterprises and municipalities can become sick or die. When we feel discomfort, we have a medical examination to find the cause. Effective treatment begins based on those results. Naturally, municipalities also require a health check-up in the form of financial analysis, but it goes without saying that the real issue is the treatment afterward. I sincerely hope that financial analysis through public accounting will be utilized in future local government management.

References
※Yubari City "Yubari City Land Suitability Plan (Material Edition)" (2021.3)

Chapter 6

Inventory of Operations and BPR

(Business Process Reengineering)

Shiga University, Koji Yokoyama

Introduction

This chapter focuses on "inventory of operations." In Chapter 2, I discussed the nature of reform and how it is conducted. The first step in the process of reform is a "current situation analysis," which includes financial analysis and inventory of operations. Financial analysis is explained in Chapter 5, so in this chapter I would like to discuss inventory of operations.

Unfortunately, just like with financial analysis, not many municipalities properly conduct an inventory of operations. In recent years, two great opportunities to conduct an inventory of operations have arisen. The first was just before the implementation of the fiscal year fixed-term staff system from fiscal 2020. Ideally, an inventory of operations should have been conducted to understand who was doing what kind of work and how much, before implementing the fiscal year fixed-term staff system. However, many municipalities simply transitioned their temporary staff to fiscal-year fixed-term staff, causing personnel costs to increase, and now some municipalities are starting to conduct an inventory of operations. It is never too late for reform, and it is something that should be done from now on. In the first place, inventory of operations should be a constant task, related not only to the introduction of the fiscal year fixed-term staff system, but also to personnel and organizational restructuring. The second opportunity is the current nationwide promotion of DX. By conducting an inventory of operations, it becomes clear which tasks require a lot of process time where many personnel are assigned, revealing where DX should be introduced. However, many municipalities do not understand that DX promotion is part of the reform process, and that inventory of operations plays an essential role. Therefore, this chapter will explain inventory of operations and business improvement.

What Is Inventory of Operations?

First, let's explore what inventory of operations means. I will introduce two well-known examples. The first example is Shizuoka Prefecture, which has been working on this since Heisei 9. The prefecture states, "The inventory of operations chart visualizes the work of the prefecture and uses the chart to improve its work." It also explains that the prefecture's work spans various fields and is very complex, and to improve the work must be organized and made visible. Hence, all the work being done is listed in the prefecture's office and organized by purpose to make it visible.

Another example is Tatebayashi City in Gunma Prefecture, where it states, "Each organization and section creates an inventory of operations chart to accurately grasp the purpose of the work, the means to achieve the purpose, and the relationship with the work." This chart enables the work to be visualized; whether the means are appropriate for the purpose can also be discerned, making it easier to improve the work. Here too, the purpose of inventory of operations is clearly stated to be business improvement.

Originally, the term inventory of operations derives from corporate management. There is an accounting term called "inventory," typically used to grasp the quantity and cost of stock. The term is applied as inventory of operations with the aim of improving the business flow. Inventory of operations involves clarifying business and unifying terminologies, going through the process of making business visible to its establishment. The original term "inventory" refers to taking goods from the shelves to check their quantity and quality, mainly performed at the fiscal year end, and it plays a key role in assessing profit and loss. Inventory of operations is the application of this inventory method to business evaluation. Specifically, it means making visible the content, type, and extent of the work being done. The principles of administrative management are the same.

In summary, inventory of operations is the organization of work by factors such as ① what kind of work exists, ② how many human resources are assigned, ③ how much time is spent, ④ how much cost is incurred, and ⑤ what procedures are being followed. The application of inventory of operations seems obvious, but how about in various municipalities? Isn't this a notably weakness seen in many public offices?

Significance and Necessity of Inventory of Operations

Next, let's discuss the significance and necessity of inventory of operations. Without inventory of operations, it is impossible to formulate comprehensive plans and administrative plans. To formulate a new plan, you first need to consider what kind of work is being done, and how the work is positioned within the municipality. Work that has fulfilled its mission must be terminated, and if there is a shortage, new work must be added. Many examples can be found where municipalities first create a comprehensive plan and then fit the work into it, but this process is backward.

Also, without inventory of operations the formation of an organization is impossible; it is not possible without understanding what kind of work is being done in which section. Proportionally, personnel management is also impossible. I believe personnel management in Japanese public offices has traditionally been weak. This can be traced back to the modern official system of the Meiji government, but the main reason today is that personnel management based on inventory of operations is not performed. Earlier, I mentioned the fiscal year fixed-term staff system, but this system cannot be introduced without first organizing who is doing what kind of work. Outsourcing is also not possible, and finally, policy evaluation and personnel evaluation cannot be conducted.

Making Business Operations Visible

What becomes clear when conducting "stock-taking of operations"? First, it reveals previously hidden tasks. Many tasks do not appear in administrative responsibility charts, organizational charts, and comprehensive plans. This is essentially an anomaly.

Second, cost-effectiveness becomes clear. For example, running high profile projects may seem glamorous, but it is only natural that they will incur heavy costs. Municipalities should discuss whether these projects are genuinely necessary at such costs. Conversely, there are tasks with no budget. Although there may be tasks that require no budget, if they involve staff essentially working for free and engaging in invisible labour, then corrections are needed. This is an issue beyond just having a low budget.

Third, inappropriate processes also become apparent. Visibility was mentioned earlier, and the main objective of stock-taking of operations is clarity. In other words, it clarifies who is conducting tasks, how they are doing it, and who is making the responsible decisions. Municipalities where scandals occur almost invariably have a problem in this regard. In municipalities where operations are visible, scandals are less likely to occur. The hotbed of scandals often involves tasks being concentrated on one person with no one checking up. If it is clear who is doing what, how they are doing it, and who is responsible, there should be fewer scandals. Since fiscal 2020, prefectures and designated cities are required to publish their internal control policies, but stock-taking of operations is also important from an internal control perspective.

Fourth, stock-taking of operations reveals overlapping or unnecessary projects. For example, when formulating a comprehensive plan, municipal employees often ask whether it is necessary to create the plan, but there is a definite need to do so. The comprehensive plan signifies a guideline for municipal policies and, simultaneously, its formulation process holds significant importance. Why? As often pointed out, an administration is compartmentalized, with various departments frequently conducting similar subsidies or projects. Integration, reorganization, discontinuation of inefficient ones, or improvements in fundamentals and methods are needed. Systematizing and organizing various policies are also essential. These actions are predicated on the stock-taking of operations.

Fifth, the need for outsourcing or RPA (Robotic Process Automation) becomes clear. When I engage in stock-taking of operations, I often encounter such cases as "Did one person handle all these tasks?" or "Was all this work done manually?" Naturally, departments operating under such conditions have extended overtime hours with employees suffering physical and mental fatigue. Even though the responsible person or department may have understood the situation and advocated for outsourcing or RPA in the past, it is often rejected by the finance department due to budget constraints. Outsourcing and RPA do indeed incur costs, but if reliance on limited staff and manual work continues indefinitely, mistakes will inevitably occur and employees will break down, a situation that affects not only public offices but also residents. Postponing tasks for the reason of no immediate budget is merely short-sighted. Stock-taking of operations is an effective means of revealing the actual burden of relevant administrative projects, and highlights the need for allocating a proper budget.

As seen above, stock-taking of operations should be considered integrally with policy evaluation and operation improvement. It is not the end goal itself but rather requisite work necessary to evaluate policies (strategies and administrative projects), improve operations, and take budgetary measures.

Flawed Inventory of Operations

Here I would like to describe some typical mistakes.

1. Never Having Conducted an Inventory of Operations: This is remarkable, but as I have said, this work is essential for human resources and budget planning.

2. Contracting a Consultant but Never Utilizing the Results: This occurs when the purpose of taking inventory is not understood. Without recognizing that improvement is the objective, it only leaves the staff burdened.

3. Positioning Considered Only in Comprehensive Planning at the Policy Evaluation Stage: This is surely odd. Local governments should not be carrying out measures that are not in the plan. New businesses must be newly positioned, and if wasteful they must be eliminated or corrected in some way.

4. Unknown Legal Basis: Many local governments do not confirm the legal basis of their operations. Most, even in terms of grants and burdens, are discretionary. Many burdens placed on prefectures and wide-area unions are often for social reasons.

5. Thinking It Is Impossible to Eliminate or Reduce Non-Mandatory Grants or Burdens: It is acceptable to scrutinize whether the ratio of burden is appropriate and whether there are merits for a local government.

6. Assuming Good Projects Do Not Cost Money: Projects that do not cost money should sometimes be stopped. Why? Because they often burden the staff. A project is not always worthwhile because it does not cost money.

7. Assuming Good Projects Are Not Local Expenditures: Even if the funding source is not a single expense, the burden of business remains, so it is necessary to examine whether the actual burden is necessary for the local government.

8. Unclear Beginning and End Dates: It is essential to set end dates. Even routine operations should be reviewed at intervals like three or five years.

9. No Discussion on Who Should Handle the Work, Regular or Temporary Staff: It is common to see the transition to temporary staff or adjustments to the number of staff without legitimate reason.

Items and Methods Required for Inventory of Operations

The necessary items for inventory of operations might include positioning in the policy system, budget positioning (general/specific sources), project cost, personnel cost, regular/non-regular staff, legal basis, and the beginning and end. The challenge is to understand the volume of work. Measuring the workload of civil servants is difficult. Factors include whether the work is specialized, core or non-core, standardized or not, timing control, and seasonality, but fundamentally it is about people × time.

Typically, understanding the workload is done by distributing questionnaires to each responsible division or staff. If you refer to Figure 6-1, you can see how labour becomes apparent when completing the matrix.

In Figure 6-1, "Administrative projects" are lined up in the left vertical column, and "Workers" in the right horizontal row. The horizontal row can be adapted as much as possible. The status and possibilities of automation (RPA) or external outsourcing (outsourcing) can also be examined. By adding working hours, overtime hours, or budgets, disparities in time, overtime, and budgets become clear. Monthly investigations also reveal monthly biases.

In the past two years, with the promotion of DX nationwide, more local governments have begun to conduct operation inventories (workload surveys), but there seem to be two major types of survey items.

[Administrative Tasks of Department X]

Task/Operator	Manager	Assistant	Person in Charge	Fiscal Year Appointed Staff	Possibility of Automation	Possibility of Outsourcing	Manual Preparedness	Others	Total
XX Event Task	○	○		○		○			● person/h
XX Contract-related Task	○	○	○				○		● person/h
XX Input-related Task				○	○		○		● person/h
...									...
Total	●●h	●●h	●●h	●●h	●●h	●●h	●●h	●●h	●●h

· The individuals involved in each administrative task, business process (approval route), automation potential, possibility of outsourcing, and policy direction become clear.
· The number of working hours and overtime hours as well as the uneven distribution of work involvement becomes clear.

Figure 6-1: Conceptual Diagram of Business Inventory (Created by the author)

I would like to emphasize to local governments the necessity of clearly defining the specific improvement objectives within the process of business enhancement when designing a survey form. As previously mentioned, there are generally two different types of distinction. Many cases have been observed where, despite the considerable burden placed on staff to fill out survey forms, the results are rendered useless as the purposes and means are misguided from the outset. A recent unfortunate example is related to the promotion of DX (digital transformation) primarily undertaken by the information system department with little communication with the reform department. Following the recommendations of the private business operator, the design of the survey form was left to the operator, and a survey corresponding to the second type mentioned earlier was conducted, but it still did not lead to reform. Even when commissioning surveys to private business operators, it is vital to thoroughly discuss the kind of reform and the items to be surveyed.

When compiling survey forms and representing various metrics (e.g., business working hours, monthly working hours, and percentage of time spent on different tasks) using graphs and charts, the intuitive perceptions of the staff are impressively reflected as objective numbers. However, the survey forms alone might not provide insights into qualitative problems, so it is advisable to conduct a survey with free descriptive questions, alongside tracking working hours and further base hearing surveys on the results for each department (responsible party). Continuous hearings can reveal the staff's true feelings that do not emerge through survey forms.

Example of BPR (Business Process Reengineering)

After organizing the survey results, it is time to think collectively about how to resolve these issues and propose business improvement plans. Conducting a survey without this process is meaningless. While business improvement is a long-standing term, "BPR" has been commonly used in recent years in the public and private sectors. Specifically, according to the Ministry of Internal Affairs and Communications, BPR stands for "Business Process Reengineering" and is defined as the practice of reducing the burden on citizens, businesses, and staff, while speeding up and improving the convenience and accuracy of business processes by understanding the challenges through detailed analysis and deriving comprehensive solutions from scratch. Some local governments may narrowly interpret BPR as being centered around PPA implementation, but as the Ministry points out, it is not merely about automation or ICT implementation, but also about overall improvements that include consolidating and simplifying procedures and documents.

Based on survey and hearing results, various outcomes are expected, but broadly speaking, the direction for improvement can be categorized as "advancement" and "efficiency." Advancement refers specifically to aligning business and HR strategies, and to planning staff and deployments based on business needs, which in administrative terms translate into policies (measures, administrative projects, etc.). Efficiency covers "abolition and simplification," such as reviewing committees, delegating authority, revising regulations, reviewing work frequency and scope; "externalization" like outsourcing administrative tasks, specialized tasks, education, and training; "standardization and consolidation" involving common vendors and suppliers, integrating business processes, rules, and forms, and standardizing local government manuals: and "automation" like introducing RPA, effectively using Excel tools, and modifying core systems.

Such categorization makes horizontal deployment possible across other city departments. Of course, the reform does not end here. It only becomes reform when the collectively devised business improvement plans are put into action. With every local government I have been involved with, the results are always reported to the executive level. The effectiveness of reform largely depends on the executive's leadership. I hope other local governments can use this chapter as a reference to initiate reform.

Work Style Reform and Internal Control Also Start with Inventory of Operations

This chapter can be summarized as follows: Inventory of operations is something that must be conducted at the outset of administrative management reform, alongside financial analysis. By conducting an inventory of operations, the subsequent review of administrative services or the direction of measures will become clear.

The national government is currently promoting work style reform. However, even if employees are instructed to take paid leave or not to work overtime, the problem will not be fundamentally resolved unless unnecessary tasks are reduced. The same goes for internal control. No matter how much surveillance is strengthened, scandals will continue to occur if the work environment that breeds misconduct is not improved. The most basic aspect is to make administrative operations more visible.

Certainly, there are challenges in understanding the operations conducted by an administration. It is not just a matter of quantity over time; there are also issues of quality. At the very least, however, the awareness and understanding of operations can lead to administrative management reform, and I feel that municipalities adopting such an attitude are proactive in both work style reform and internal control. It is my belief that municipalities intending to conduct these reforms should first perform an inventory of operations.

References

※Shizuoka Prefecture, "Operation Inventory Table" (2017)
※Tatebayashi City, "Operation Inventory Table" (2019)
※Deloitte Tohmatsu Consulting LLC, Takashi Ono et al., "The Textbook of Human Resource Transformation to Build the Strongest Organization" (Japan Productivity Center, 2019)

Chapter 7

Digital Transformation Promotion Plan

within Local Governments

KKC Information Systems Corporation - Akiyuki Sannomiya

Introduction

In this chapter I will introduce local government DX. The term "DX" has become increasingly common in recent years. Here I want to explain the meaning and necessity of DX as well as the methods of promotion by local governments, and the kind of future we can envision, from the perspectives of both residents and local governments.

What Is DX?

DX or DIE, reminiscent of "Dead or Alive," is now a buzz phrase for "live or die." Do we engage in DX and survive, or do we fade away and disappear? I hope you will consider the importance of initiating the first step toward DX as the wave of digital revolution sweeps over us.

DX is an abbreviation for "digital transformation." It could have been "DT," but in English-speaking countries, the symbol "X" is commonly used to represent "trans," hence "DX."

The concept of DX was proposed in 2004 by Erik Stolterman, a professor in Sweden at the time. In Japan, the circulation of DX began with the Ministry of Economy, Trade and Industry's "DX Report" issued in 2018. DX translated directly means "digital change or transformation," but its essence is "using digital technology to enrich people's lives, changing and continuing to change for the better." Introducing tools or products to facilitate DX is hardly a mistake, but the crux of local government DX is whether it "benefits the residents."

The momentum towards DX captures the processes of "digitization" and "digitalization." Digitization refers to converting from analog to digital, for example, turning paper into PDF data or using a smartphone or digital camera instead of a film camera. Digitalization means changing systems or processes to achieve greater efficiency, such as digitizing and sharing meeting materials instead of copying and distributing them, allowing participants to review them in advance (simplification and efficiency). One step beyond "digitalization" is digital transformation, or changing and creating new value and values while making processes more efficient. "The world is changed by people thinking outside the box." Private companies are now adopting this perspective in their hiring practices.

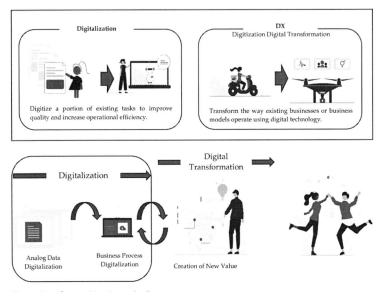

Figure 7-1 (Created by the author)

National Policies

Japan's priority plan for a digital society includes digital growth strategies and the call for "BPR" (Business Process Reengineering = Business Reform) and regulatory reform (Figure 7-2). The goal is to create a social infrastructure where every citizen can choose from diverse services that best suit their needs.

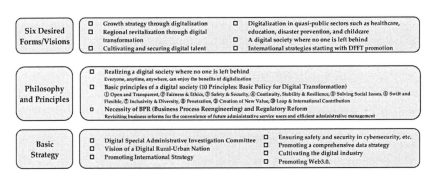

Six Desired Forms/Visions	□ Growth strategy through digitalization □ Regional revitalization through digital transformation □ Cultivating and securing digital talent	□ Digitalization in quasi-public sectors such as healthcare, education, disaster prevention, and childcare □ A digital society where no one is left behind □ International strategies starting with DFFT promotion
Philosophy and Principles	□ Realizing a digital society where no one is left behind Everyone, anytime, anywhere, can enjoy the benefits of digitalization □ Basic principles of a digital society (10 Principles: Basic Policy for Digital Transformation) ① Open and Transparent, ② Fairness & Ethics, ③ Safety & Security, ④ Continuity, Stability & Resilience, ⑤ Solving Social Issues, ⑥ Swift and Flexible, ⑦ Inclusivity & Diversity, ⑧ Penetration, ⑨ Creation of New Value, ⑩ Leap & International Contribution □ Necessity of BPR (Business Process Reengineering) and Regulatory Reform Revisiting business reforms for the convenience of future administrative service users and efficient administrative management		
Basic Strategy	□ Digital Special Administrative Investigation Committee □ Vision of a Digital Rural-Urban Nation □ Promoting International Strategy	□ Ensuring safety and security in cybersecurity, etc. □ Promoting a comprehensive data strategy □ Cultivating the digital industry □ Promoting Web3.0.

Figure 7-2 (Created by the author)

Other DX-related materials include the Digital Government Execution Plan, Growth Strategy Execution Plan, and Declaration of the Creation of the World's Most Advanced Digital Nation & Government and Private Sector Data Utilization Promotion Basic Plan. In summary, these materials emphasize that serious consequences can be expected if we do not undergo DX by 2025, specifically, ① a decrease in work efficiency and ② the occurrence of massive economic losses.

① Decrease in work efficiency: The Ministry of Internal Affairs and Communications' Information and Communication White Paper predicts a decrease in the working-age population (ages 15-64) from 73 million in 2020 to 70 million in 2025, and to 63 million in 2035. These decreases of 430,000 in three years and about 10 million in fifteen years represent an unprecedented pace of aging and population decline.

② Massive economic losses: The Ministry of Economy, Trade and Industry estimates an annual loss of 12 trillion yen. The current economic loss is said to be about 4 trillion yen, so imagine a loss three times higher. To solve these problems, we need IT to reform and streamline work.

In a survey of 193 United Nations member states published by the UN in July 2020, Japan ranked 14th, still high but down four places from the previous survey, clearly indicating a degree of stagnation in transitioning to a digital society. In the OECD's online administrative procedures survey of 30 participating countries, Japan's online utilization rate was the lowest at 7.3 percent. In response to this result, the Cabinet Office listed two challenges in its Annual Economic and Fiscal Report in November 2020: ① Shortage of human resources to drive digitalization and ② Concentration of human resources for digitalization in the IT industry, with fewer workers in the public sector including administration. In short, the overall view is that "Japan lacks strong digital talent."

Changes Surrounding Local Governments

Japan's current population stands at roughly 123 million. Between 2021 and 2022, the nation's population contracted by about 620,000 people, marking the 13th consecutive year of decline. According to the Regional Economic Analysis System (RESAS), Shiga Prefecture has experienced a gradual decline since 2020. Notably, the working-age population is forecasted to fall by 153,000 over the next 25 years. Although the overall population in the prefecture will decrease by about 10 percent, the working-age population, which bears the heaviest societal load, will drop by nearly 20 percent. Even in Shiga Prefecture, where the population decline is gradual, economic and social infrastructure difficulties are on the horizon.

The memorable Special Fixed Amount Benefit Program (100,000 yen per person) promised prompt payment through online application using the "My Number Card" system. However, incorrect entries and double applications led many local governments to halt online applications, resorting back to paper forms. In the analog process, the Nishinomiya City Health Center accidentally sent the personal information of COVID-19 patients to private residences via fax, twice. To overcome such issues, digital legal development is progressing.

The Administrative Procedure Online Act was enacted in 2004, making possible online use by administrative agencies. The Digital Procedure Act of 2019 mandates online implementation for ministries and prefectures, while local governments are obliged to make efforts. The three basic principles of digitization are as follows.

1. Digital First: Completing procedures digitally without using paper.
2. Once Only: Not requiring applicants to provide the same information repeatedly by coordinating data at the back-office side.
3. Connected One-Stop: Connecting not only administrative agencies but also utilities, private companies, etc., to complete multiple procedures at one stop.

The "Digital Rural-Urban Nation Concept" aims to cover regional and urban disparities through digital technology, enabling high-quality living, work, and leisure in rural areas. Subsidies have been prepared for the realization of technology in the internet environment, transportation, medical care, and education.

Definition of Local Government DX

The significance of local government DX varies, but generally it is defined as "transforming administrative services using digital technology." Another perspective emphasizes "improving the convenience of residents." In other words, if it is not resident-centric, no matter the digital technology used, it is not local government DX. Alongside the vulnerabilities in communication infrastructure, information bases, and data utilization revealed during the pandemic, it is important not to solely rely on technology while using it effectively.

Outline of the Local Government DX Promotion Plan

Numerous materials on DX have been published by the Ministry of Internal Affairs and Communications, but I would like to expand on the Outline of the Local Government DX Promotion Plan dated December 25, 2020, and the Local Government DX Promotion Procedures dated July 7, 2021, taking into account the definition of local government DX.

Both documents clearly state ① "By when," ② "How." and ③ "What needs to be done."

① By when: By March 2026, aligning with the "2025 cliff" proposed by the Ministry of Economy, Trade, and Industry.

② How: By establishing an organizational structure to promote DX. It is crucial to organize entities that can drive initiatives, not only by recruiting digitally proficient workers but also by fostering talents from current human resources to ensure strategic advancement.

③ What needs to be done: This is explicitly outlined in six key areas:
i) Standardizing and unifying the core systems for personal information administrative use.
ii) Promoting the widespread adoption of the My Number Card system.
iii) Enabling online utilization of administrative procedures such as notices and application forms.
iv) Reassessing business processes and advocating the introduction and utilization of AI (Artificial Intelligence) and RPA (Robotic Process Automation).
v) Encouraging the introduction and use of teleworking as part of work style reform.
vi) Conducting a thorough review of appropriate policies and ensuring robust security measures in line with the revised security policy guidelines.

Two other crucial initiatives to be concurrently pursued include the digitalization of local communities and measures against the "digital divide." The term digital divide refers to the disparity between those who can benefit from digital resources and those who cannot, with measures aimed at bridging the gap.

Now I will delve into and explain the three major points of our initiative.

1. Standardization/Unification of Core Systems for Personal Information Management

Across approximately 1,700 municipalities nationwide, various administrative systems are in operation. Standardization and unification bring advantages that include uniformity in modification costs across municipalities during system reform and seamless data collaboration through the use of common infrastructure. The targeted tasks include 20 tasks closely tied to residents' lives, promising reduced waiting times for residents and decreased administrative burdens for municipalities. Preparations are also underway for what is called Government Cloud, or "Gov-Cloud," a framework in which 20 task systems in cassette form make it virtually possible to allocate personal resident tax to Company A, child allowances to Company B, or welfare assistance to Company C. A common platform controls different business systems to facilitate collaboration, with each system loaded onto this common platform.

【Government Cloud】

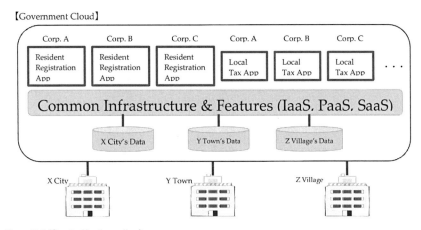

Figure 7-3 (Created by the author)

Towards standardization and unification, municipalities must formulate new system functional specifications, compare old and new system functionalities (FIT & GAP), and develop system migration plans as immediate needs. From FY2023 onwards, there is a need to systematically proceed with infrastructure planning, character identification, data cleansing, non-standardized system coordination checks, and migration rehearsals to new systems, while anticipating personnel requirements.

2. Promotion of My Number Card Distribution

Reasons for the slow dissemination of My Number Card include the extremely limited places of use, anxiety about possession, complicated application and receiving procedures, and possible identity verification without the card. As of July 30, 2022, the national average distribution rate was 45.9 percent, with Shiga Prefecture ranking 6th, Aichi Prefecture 16th, and Gifu Prefecture 32nd. In June 2022, the government was reported to reflect the My Number issuance rate in local allocation taxes. Unless card use becomes more widespread, administrative procedures will remain unchanged, and in-office procedures will continue to be basic, regardless of the infrastructure or services provided. The government has therefore included in its policy framework the intention to eliminate and integrate paper insurance cards into the My Number Card system. Despite its pros and cons, the distribution rate of My Number Card is set to skyrocket under the policy of mandatory principles. Also, integration with driving licenses is now scheduled two years earlier by the end of FY2024. Future considerations include mobile driving licenses on smartphones (already implemented in the U.S., Finland, and Thailand).

3. Utilization of Administrative Procedures Such as Notifications and Applications Online
Thirty-one administrative procedures, excluding those for automobiles, can be accessed using My Number Card from "My Portal" in municipalities. Child allowance, childcare support allowance notifications, nursing care or support application, and others services are also included. Though variations may exist across municipalities, with general procedures numbering 3,000-5,000, prioritizing these procedures for online conversion based on user perspectives is deemed best.

Other focal initiatives include AI/RPA, sharing the common point of "automation through data utilization." For example, complex nursery admissions requiring time and certain judgments and rules can now be assigned in seconds with AI. RPA automates routine administrative tasks like data entry and processing. However, many municipalities have not reached full utilization due to invisible work processes and insufficient inventory of operations, despite acquiring the products and tools. First, sufficient time must be allocated to "inventory" in order to understand the current situation, and execution must follow based on a visualized plan. Telework has reached 100 percent in prefectures and government-designated cities, and about 50 percent in other municipalities, though currently limited to specific departments or divisions. In security, policy reviews must be conducted with ongoing security enhancements. While synchronization between DX promotion and security measures is absolutely necessary, specialized knowledge is required, so hiring external specialists or considering outsourcing is also effective.

Leading Examples

- Example 1 (Estonia): Estonia, a globally advanced nation in Northern Europe with a population of around 1.3 million, is a trailblazer in electronic government and e-governance. Under administrative guidance, each citizen is assigned a national ID number (eID), allowing access to personal information such as name, date of birth, address, tax amount, educational background, medical history, criminal record, and more through their personal portal. Also, online procedures for changing address update the data with utility companies, banks, telecommunications companies, and other service providers (Connected One-Stop). Non-digital procedures include marriage, divorce, and real estate sales; requiring careful consideration, these procedures are intentionally carried out offline (in person).

• Example 2 (Mita City, Hyogo Prefecture): In Japan, an example can be seen in Mita City, Hyogo Prefecture. Faced with a population outflow, especially among residents in their 20s relocating to places like Osaka, Kobe, Nishinomiya, and Amagasaki, the city has presented the "Mita Satoyama Smart City Concept" as part of its efforts to "build a town unwilling to lose to population decline." Embracing the inevitability of population decline, the aim is to create a city where by leveraging digital technology even the elderly can live comfortably. There are also many collaboration agreements with various companies and universities, including Marubeni, Kansai Electric Power, and local bus companies.

• Example 3 (Kitami City, Hokkaido): Kitami City in Hokkaido is a well-known local government model that began implementing "workcations" before the term became widespread in Japan as well as challenging various regional issues such as work style reform, personnel recruitment and training, and U-turn support. Notably, their "Resident-Centered DX" initiative, launched in 2009, offers a "no-writing counter" and "one-stop comprehensive counter service." With the elimination of the once-crowded writing desk, municipal staff enter the necessary information on a tablet to produce application, notification and other forms. Residents only need to sign to complete the procedures. The comprehensive counter has expanded in a planned way, starting with the municipal and tax divisions, to include various other services. For condolences procedures, the dedicated "Condolences One-Stop" counter handles 54 types of reception and 10 types of guidance.

• Example 4 (Yabu City, Hyogo Prefecture): Yabu City in Hyogo Prefecture has launched a virtual city hall in the metaverse to implement regional revitalization measures with the aim of increasing its population through new forms of attractive promotions, tourism PR, interaction bases, and more.

• Example 5 (Cashless Payment): The issuance of cashless window certificates is rapidly being introduced across municipalities nationwide. With the utilization of credit cards, transportation IC cards, and smartphone payment platforms such as PayPay, LINE Pay, and d-payment, resident do not need to carry cash, and administrations benefit from eliminating cash loss and reducing problems and errors in handling change.

Future Prospects

In private sector management, the three principles of management resources were once said to be "people, goods, and money." In recent years, "digital technology," including information and data, has become an essential factor, surpassing in weight the traditional three management resources. This is also true for local governments. Next, I will outline the key points for promoting local government DX based on administrative reform.

1. Building a Cross-Sectional System: In line with the Digital Agency's philosophy, it is important to create a system where information and opinions are not just vertically divided but flow laterally as well.

2. Securing & Nurturing Digital Talent: IT-literate personnel need to be cultivated constantly to keep up with the overwhelmingly rapid progression of today's digital society.

3. Planned Initiatives: While utilizing tangible assets like people, goods, and money, and the intangible assets of DX, it is essential to realize that tangible resources are limited. As described in the leading examples above, not every detail was digitized all at once; the process of short- and long-term actions requires careful planning.

4. Strengthening Inter-Municipal Collaboration: There are stories of success and failure that need to be shared among municipalities to enhance relationships and cooperation beyond the current level. By doing so, we can envision the true form of administration that should be in place 10, 20, or 50 years in the future, and see a sustainable future.

In conclusion, the explanations provided within the confines of these pages represent only a fraction of the directions in which nations and administrations should be moving. In an era where waves of disruptive innovations are sweeping over us, the mindset of each individual becomes crucial. Your first step towards innovation starts with questioning traditional practices, asking "Why?" and "How?" We look forward to your contributions in envisioning the Future of Local Government Digital Transformation (DX) and actively working towards promoting regional economies and addressing the many challenges.

References

※Ministry of Internal Affairs and Communications website, "Status of My Number Card Issuance," link (accessed on July 30, Reiwa 4)

※Ministry of Internal Affairs and Communications website, "Information and Communication White Paper for Reiwa 4 Fiscal Year," link (accessed in July, Reiwa 4)

※Ministry of Internal Affairs and Communications website, "Local Government Digital Transformation (DX) Promotion Plan," "Local Government DX Promotion Procedures," and "Digital Government Implementation Plan," link (accessed on December 25, Reiwa 2)

※Ministry of Economy, Trade, and Industry website, "DX Report – Overcoming the '2025 Cliff,' IT System, and Full-scale Deployment of DX," link (accessed on September 7, Heisei 30)

※Government CIO Portal, "Results of Administrative Procedure Inventory, Etc.," link (accessed on April 2, Reiwa 2)

※Government CIO Portal, "Utilization of Government Cloud by Local Governments (Draft)," link (accessed in August, Reiwa 3)

※United Nations website, "E-Government Survey 2020," link (accessed on July 10, Reiwa 2)

※Cabinet Office website, "Annual Economic and Fiscal Report," link (accessed in November, Reiwa 2)

※Sanda City, Hyogo Prefecture website link (accessed in July, Reiwa 4)

※Yabu City, Hyogo Prefecture website link (accessed in July, Reiwa 4)

※Seed Planning Inc., Digital Administration, link (accessed in July, Reiwa 4)

※Kobe Newspaper website link (accessed on August 15, Reiwa 2)

Note: Reiwa is the current era name in Japan. Reiwa 4 corresponds to 2022 in the Gregorian calendar. Heisei 30 corresponds to 2018 in the Gregorian calendar.

Chapter 8

Review of Expenditures Such as Subsidies and

Burden Charges

Shiga University, Koji Yokoyama

Introduction

I discussed the overall review of administrative activities in Chapter 4, but a more meticulous method would divide the topic into categories, including "reviewing expenditures such as grants and burden charges," "reviewing revenues like usage fees and handling fees," "reviewing public facilities," "reviewing the Designated Administrator System and private-sector vitality," or further examining details based on individual groups or event projects.

In this chapter I would like to discuss the review of "grants, burden charges, and entrusted expenses," which is in particularly high demand within the "review of administrative activities." Many local government policies involve the expenditure of grants, burden charges, and entrusted expenses. Thus, reviewing these expenditures occupies a significant weight in administrative management reform.

Unfortunately, however, examples can be found where local government employees execute grants, burden charges, and entrusted expenses without properly understanding their distinctions. In this chapter I will first explain grants, burden charges, and entrusted expenses, and then discuss specific perspectives on reviewing grants.

Differences and Basis for Subsidies, Burden Charges, and Entrusted Expenses

First, let's take a textbook view of grants. Grants are monetary benefits provided by local governments to private individuals for specific administrative purposes, and are permitted when deemed necessary for the public interest. The legal basis of grants can be traced back to the Constitution. Article 94 of the Constitution states, "Local governments shall manage their property, conduct business, and execute administration, and may enact ordinances within the scope of the law." In other words, local governments are constitutionally guaranteed the right to manage and dispose of property in the same way as individuals, and this includes the disbursement of grants. At the same time, Article 89 states, "No public money or other property shall be expended or appropriated for the use, benefit, or maintenance of any religious organization or charitable, educational or benevolent enterprises not under the control of public authority," thus restricting the expenditure of public funds for private religious, charity, educational, and other enterprises. Specifically, the latter is aimed at "preventing the misuse of public funds and ensuring the neutrality of the state" based on reflections of the nation's pre-war totalitarianism. However, some municipal officials misinterpret the concept of "support but no control," erroneously thinking they can provide grants without interference. The meaning of support but no control is there should be no control over the sovereignty of an organization through the provision of grants, not that ambiguous grants can be provided without proper inspection or auditing by the municipality. This is not equivalent to extraterritoriality and should be clearly understood as such.

The constitutional basis is as stated above. The direct basis is Article 232-2 of the Local Autonomy Act, which states, "Ordinary local public entities may make donations or grants if they deem it necessary for the public interest." In turn, whether it is necessary for the public interest is determined by the municipality's head and assembly in each individual case, but this is not an entirely discretionary act and must be objectively recognized as necessary to the public interest. On the actual local government scene, there are "mandatory grants" based on individual laws and "discretionary grants" without a legal basis. In Yokohama City, the grant is defined as "discretionary spending to subsidize specific projects or activities that, although not stipulated by law, etc., are deemed necessary for the public interest in promoting or fostering coordination projects with the country or other local public entities, or highly necessary policies that the city should bear." Most local governments struggle with discretionary grants. The details of this review will be described later.

Also, related laws include the Law Concerning the Proper Execution of Budgets Related to Grants, etc. (commonly referred to as the Grant Properness Act) (Showa 30 Act No. 179). While not a lengthy law, it does define the procedures related to grant distribution, including "definition," "application," "decision," "performance report," "cancellation of decision," "return," and "on-site inspection." The essence of grants, such as "purpose," "target," "start-end period," and "outcome," can be seen in this law. However, the law applies to grants disbursed from national to local public entities, not those disbursed from local public entities. Therefore, it is common for each local public entity to establish Grant Distribution Ordinances, Grant Distribution Regulations, or Grant Distribution Guidelines in accordance with this law. Occasionally, when I enter a municipality to review their grants and burden charges, I find there are no distribution regulations or guidelines, and that is an immediate disqualification. Grants without distribution guidelines should not exist.

In terms of burden charges, according to the Local Finance Small Dictionary, burden charges are monetary benefits where those with special interest in certain projects bear all or part of the costs required to implement the project, in accordance with the degree of benefit received from its implementation. There are cases where the ratio of expense burden for certain projects is determined from a financial policy perspective or other viewpoints. The former is imposed by national and local public entities on citizens or residents and requires a legal basis. The latter is found between national and local public entities, or between local public entities, and may also be called shared charges. Specific laws include Article 58 of the Road Act, Article 61 of the Road Act, Article 75 of the City Planning Act, Article 33 of the Coastal Act, Article 18 of the Sewerage Act, Article 18-2 of the Sewerage Act, Article 67 of the River Act, and Article 224 of the Local Autonomy Act.

The above was an explanation of mandatory levies or "obligatory levies" based on legal provisions, but at the actual local government level, there are also "discretionary levies" akin to subsidies. Yokohama City defines this as "discretionary expenditures to cover membership fees or actual costs of specific projects or activities conducted by the nation, local governments, organizations composed of local governments, private organizations, etc., from which the city derives special benefits, regardless of whether or not there is continuity." Similar to subsidies, this discretionary levy is problematic in many local governments. We often observe it being used for expenses related to events or committee-style execution, where it is spent as if it were a subsidy without understanding its true meaning, burdening not only the finances but also local government staff.

We must ascertain whether the nature of the expenditure aligns more appropriately with subsidies or levies. Next, regarding commission fees, according to the Local Finance Dictionary, commission fees are expenses paid as counter-remuneration when a local public body entrusts others with business or projects that fall under its jurisdiction without directly implementing them. They are recorded as "commission charges" in the budget. Commissions are conducted through public law based on legal provisions and private law contracts without legal provisions. Both generally require entering a commission contract. Examples include collection and payment of collected securities, collection or receipt of fees and charges, entrusting expenditures, management entrustment to the public bodies of public facilities, and commissioning of tasks. In private law commissions, methods are employed that are advantageous and effective, such as tests, inspections, research, and other tasks that mainly require specialized skills or knowledge, statistical surveys, design, surveying, observation, and film/television productions.

Even with commission fees, just like with the previously mentioned subsidies and levies, thoughtless spending in regions or by organizations can lead to trouble with residents who may claim the administration should be handling these tasks. Internal discussions within the local government regarding the nature of fiscal engagement in policy system design are required, with carefully debate and planning on whether subsidies, levies, or commission fees are the most appropriate methods.

Classification of Subsidies

Next, subsidies can be classified in several ways. First, are they obligatory subsidies or discretionary subsidies? Those determined by law are obligatory, while the rest are discretionary. When reviewing subsidies and levies, the obligatory ones with legal obligations might be exempted. Discretionary subsidies are usually the primary target, but there may be room for discussion regarding the ratio or procedures of obligatory subsidies.

Another way to classify subsidies is whether they are single or collaborative subsidies. Though single subsidies are the primary focus, collaborative ones also need to be considered. There are often cases where they are overlooked in financial assessments, arguing it is acceptable since the nation or prefecture is partially funding them, but discussions are needed on whether collaboration is necessary or if the burden ratio is appropriate.

Furthermore, some local governments classify subsidies by nature or type. Taga Town in Shiga Prefecture classifies subsidies as operational cost or project cost subsidies. Kobe City classifies them as economic support type (often related to welfare), event support type, facility development support type, administrative supplementary type, and policy guidance type.

This kind of classification helps identify where subsidies are concentrated and allows for goal setting when compressing finances. Since subsidies vary widely, local governments should decide on the appropriate classification based on the perspective they want to review at that time.

Effects and Issues of Subsidies

As for the effects and issues of subsidies, the effects include revitalizing community activities, stimulating economic activities, promoting town development, and complementing administrative roles.

On the other hand, the main issues can be broken down into four areas: ① If not strategically allocated, the effects are invisible. Similar to the explanation of administrative projects, subsidies provided without a purpose, goal, target, or other basic perspectives are simply a waste of taxpayers' money. ② Subsidies once granted become vested interests, and it is rare for organizations to voluntarily decline money once received. There are limits to budgets, and prioritization based on proper criteria is necessary to implement a scrap-and-build approach. ③ Projects that should be handled by the administration are easily carried out through subsidy expenditures. This applies not only to subsidies but also levies and commission fees. Local governments occasionally appear indifferent once the money is provided, but spending subsidies does not absolve an administrative of its responsibility. Public and private sectors should work together for community betterment, first discussing what the administration and policy should do, then considering subsidies and other methods. ④ At worst, subsidies can lead to scandals or financial deterioration—just like overall administrative reform, improper execution of subsidies and other financial measures inevitably leads to scandals and a waste of tax money. In an era when most local governments are facing financial hardships, there is no room for improper spending of subsidies and the like.

Perspectives on Reconsidering Subsidies

First, let's discuss the perspectives from which we should review these subsidies, and outline several points. Subsidies in the following conditions should be abolished or amended.

1. Lack of System Utilization: There are two conceivable reasons for this situation. One is the lack of demand, which means the system should have been eliminated in the first place. The other is where existing demand is stifled by a user-unfriendly system leading to no applications. This may occur when the applicants are limited to specific organizations, such as community associations or merchant associations, or when the subsidy rate is too low, resulting in a high self-pay burden. In these cases, improvements should be made to simplify the application process.

2. Mismatch with Social Conditions or Municipal Policies: Some policies were created decades ago and may have already fulfilled their mission.

3. Small Subsidy Amount Relative to Total Revenue: This situation includes cases where wealthy businesses or organizations receive subsidies as small as 10,000 yen; they might not need the subsidy, but continue to receive it as there is no reason to refuse it.

4. Carryover Funds Exceeding Subsidy Amounts: Fund carryover is common, and in se-

vere cases, the received subsidy is carried over to the next fiscal year. Such organizations do not need subsidies.

5. Supplementing National or Prefectural Subsidies for Organization Operation, but Generating Carryover Funds that Exceed City Subsidy Amounts: Organizations may receive subsidies from the prefecture and various other places, increasing the carryover of funds. This may not be necessary either.

6. Large Municipal Burden for Subsidy Project Expenses: This case refers to organizations refusing a project without first receiving a subsidy or claiming hardship without it. If merely for their own satisfaction, they should stop doing it.

7. Overlap with Other Subsidies Provided by the Municipality: This situation is also common, especially in welfare and commercial industries.

8. Lack of Guidelines, Regulations, and Agreements: This lack is unacceptable without a legal basis, or if guidelines have not been revised in decades. Guidelines and such should be reviewed flexibly according to the times.

9. High Subsidy Amount without a Defined Grant Limit: This case is also common, especially with long-standing organization subsidies. A maximum amount must be established.

10. Complex Procedures That Are Unintelligible to Applicants: This aspect is crucial. If a subsidy is not being used, it should be stopped and the problem investigated. If procedures are cumbersome, they should be simplified.

11. Expenditures Not Aligned with the Stipulated Purpose and Eligible Expenses in the Grant Guidelines: This case is common with organizational subsidies. Recently there has been a shift to specific project cost subsidies.

12. Granting Subsidies Every Year with an Unclear Basis for the Cumulative Amount: This case is also being revised recently. For example, having the same subsidy amount like 50,000 yen every year is unusual and can lead to scandals if the amount is not thoroughly calculated.

The above twelve cases are specific examples of review perspectives. Common criteria are needed to review the selected projects fairly. Let's look at some concrete examples.

Standards for Subsidy Evaluation

The first criterion is "public interest." It is essential to determine whether there is a high demand for the subsidy, whether it aligns with the local government's policies, and whether it contributes to the residents' welfare.

The second criterion is "fairness and transparency." It is unacceptable for a grant to be consistently allocated to a particular organization. For instance, automatically disbursing funds to the same group annually without undergoing a proper evaluation is inappropriate. Evaluation and selection are vital before decisions are made.

The third criterion is the "need for administrative involvement." Whether the need for administrative support is genuine or the target organization can operate independently or be replaced by another private organization should be assessed. A related issue arises when an organization's administrative office is situated within the local government's premises, effectively allowing the local governmental staff to manage the organization's affairs. This setup should generally be avoided, as the same official granting funds to an organization and also managing its affairs, even going as far as preparing activity reports for the local government, presents a problematic situation that can often lead to improprieties.

The fourth criterion is "grant effectiveness." It is crucial to evaluate whether the grant is achieving its anticipated effects, benefitting the wider population, and not unfairly favoring a select few. If the expected outcomes are not being achieved, it may be necessary to reconsider the grant itself.

The fifth criterion is "validity," which involves assessing whether the grant's amount and rate are reasonable; whether the targeted expenses and basis for calculation are clear; whether the contribution is essential; and whether the cost-sharing ratio is appropriate. Kobe City, for instance, also considers factors such as priority in terms of importance and effectiveness of the methods used. It is important to evaluate the financial situation of the grant-receiving organization as well. Many local governments might grant funds and consider the matter closed. Although they may receive performance reports, they often lack comprehensive knowledge about the organization's operations. It is essential to check the appropriateness of the organizations receiving public funds, and if suspicions arise, funding should be reconsidered.

In summary, the four main considerations are (1) appropriateness of the objective, (2) suitability of the means and methods, (3) efficacy of the initiative, and (4) suitability of the target organization. The specific details and criteria may vary and should be tailored according to the circumstances of each local government.

Perspectives on Rationalizing Subsidies

From the perspectives previously outlined, I would like to discuss various points regarding subsidies, specifically the need for review and how to improve them.

First is the rationalization of subsidy amounts and rates that involves considering their appropriateness. Sometimes authorities that have previously reviewed subsidies may have strict standards, such as requiring the subsidy to be no more than half or, in more severe cases, less than one-third. While this is not necessarily wrong, I think it is worthwhile reconsidering. For a good project and recipient, even a 100 percent subsidy might be acceptable. Securing half the amount through self-funding is a tremendous task. I wonder if it is necessary to strictly adhere to the one-half figure. However, it should not become a vested right that continues year after year.

Second is the subsidies for the operation of organizations. It may be case by case, but in my experience it is better to withdraw assistance. It is not appropriate to lackadaisically grant hundreds of thousands or tens of thousands to an organization. I think it is better to build up the project cost, even if it takes time.

Third, in terms of transitioning to appropriate spending methods, we need to consider whether subsidies are the best form in the first place. Options such as direct execution by the administration or outsourcing could be considered.

Fourth is the rationalization of recipient selection. Public recruitment is the main principle for selecting recipients. Most subsidies that become vested rights are non-public, granted annually to certain organizations without a selection review. This is commonly found with subsidies granted to social education-related organizations. Although not all of it is wrong, traditional organizations cannot deny having benefited in the past. If a truly needed organization applies, it will pass the review. Organizations that reject public recruitment and review have often enjoyed benefits without any effort.

Fifth is verification of the financial situation of the subsidy recipients, which involves looking at carried-over funds, internal reserves, dependence on subsidies, and others. In some cases, most of the subsidies granted become tributes to upper-level entities in the prefecture or country. There are many actual examples where it seems the recipient organizations only exist to pay these tributes. These examples are found in various fields and not just social education, and should be reviewed in your municipalities. There should be examples aplenty. Most are unobligated burdens that I think should be stopped, and include associations and liaison councils.

Lastly is the prohibition of secondary subsidization, where the recipient organization provides subsidies to another organization. In general, this should not be allowed, except in extreme cases, as it often leads to inefficiency.

Recommendation of Segment-by-Segment Review

As described above, I recommend assessing subsidies based on the standards and perspectives for review. In actual reviews I urge a segment by segment approach, as shown in Figure 8-1. Especially for subsidies like the detailed Social Welfare Council Subsidy, it is necessary to break down the contents. Basically, by completing a matrix like the one used in the "shelving business," the reality becomes clearer.

In the example, "Business & Activities" is aligned in the left vertical column and "Districts" in the right horizontal row in order to verify whether businesses and activities are conducted appropriately in each district. If an activity is carried out in District A but not in District C, you investigate why. If there is no demand in District C, then the reason is valid. If there is a need not being met, then there is a problem. By adding budget information, budget bias also becomes clear. Through this process, scandals may be revealed. For instance, the activity in District B might be reported in the project plan or performance report but never actually conducted, with local officials embezzling the subsidy.

Even if not a scandal, a segment-by-segment subsidy review can scrutinize the bias where a large budget is invested in unnecessary areas and vice versa. Proper budget compilation also becomes possible. A true budget review is simply an appropriate distribution of the budget. An arbitrary review like a uniform 10 percent cut is often carried out, but the roughness of this method cannot be denied. Only by reviewing segment by segment can a real budget review be achieved.

【Subsidy Name】 ex.) Social Welfare Council Subsidy

Activity by Type/Area	Region A	Region B	Region C	...	Total
○○ Salon Business	○	△	×		30,000
Elderly Monitoring Activity	△	○	×		50,000
Child Monitoring Activity	×	△	○		20,000
...					
Total	50,000	70,000	10,000		

Traditionally, decisions are based only on the total amount, making it difficult to conduct a thorough review.

Disparities among different businesses become clear.

Regional disparities become clear.

Proper business execution and the prevention of misconduct are promoted.

Figure 8-1. Conceptual Diagram of Grant Revisions by Segment (Created by the author)

Framework and Format for the Revision of Subsidies

The framework and format for the revision of subsidies are fundamentally based on the framework and format for the revision of administrative projects discussed in Chapter 4. However, I would like to emphasize four particular points.

First, similar to the framework for the revision of administrative projects, reviews must be conducted through an organization or institution directly under the jurisdiction of the administration head who combines both authority and expertise, akin to a task force. A system that clearly explains to the legislature and discloses to the public should be adopted.

Second, it is crucial to establish rational, objective, and unified criteria to ensure a fair review. Exceptions that apply only to specific organizations or exclude others must never be created. Such actions will cause trust in reform to be lost forever.

Third, similar to the format for the revision of administrative projects, the format for the revision of subsidies should be simple and reduce the burden on both evaluators and evaluatees as much as possible. Finally, it is impossible to review the enormous number of subsidies in a single fiscal year. Reviewing over multiple years is an acceptable method. Moreover, the review does not end once it is done as continuous revision is necessary. I hope reviews will become part of the standard organizational culture according to social conditions.

References

※Nobuo Ishihara, Akira Shimazu (Supervised), "Local Finance Mini Dictionary" (Gyosei, 2011)
※Yokohama City General Affairs Bureau Work Reform Division, "Guidelines on the Review of Burden Money, Subsidies, and Grants" (Feb 2015)
※Taga Town, "Subsidy Review Guidelines" (2018)
※Kobe City, "Subsidy Review Guidelines" (2016)
※Konan City, "Subsidy Review Committee Materials" (2019)

Chapter 9

Revision of Usage Fees and Administrative Fees

Tax Accountant, Kazuo Kondo

Introduction

Local government services aim to enhance the welfare of residents, funded primarily by tax revenue and government subsidies. Among the many administrative services offered, some are specifically enjoyed by particular residents. Covering these services entirely through tax revenue creates unfairness among residents depending on the frequency of use. Thus, for administrative services that benefit identifiable recipients, it is possible to charge corresponding fees and administrative fees. This chapter discusses the basic principles of usage fees and administrative fees, and highlights the points to consider when calculating or revising these fees.

Usage Fees and Administrative Fees

The basis for collecting usage fees and administrative fees is prescribed in the Local Autonomy Act. Usage fees are specified in Article 225, stating, "Ordinary local public bodies may charge usage fees for the use of administrative property or public facilities as permitted under the provisions of Article 238-4, paragraph 7 (regarding the management and disposition of administrative property)." Examples include the use of civic halls, meeting rooms, and public swimming pools. Administrative fees, as prescribed in the same law's Article 227, may be collected "by the ordinary local public body for the benefit of a specific individual." Examples include the issuance fees for residence and income certificates.

The fundamental concepts of usage fees and administrative fees can be summarized in three points.

1. Principle of Beneficiary Pays: Unlike taxes, appropriate charges are necessary for specific citizens for specific purposes.

2. Ensuring Fairness and Transparency: Being a public service using public assets, charges must be clear and not favor specific beneficiaries.

3. Coordination between Similar Facilities: For facilities like community centers used mainly by local residents, it is important to avoid regional disparities and set proper fees in comparison with neighboring or similar facilities, both public and private.

Methods of Calculating Usage Fees

The opportunities for calculating usage fees include new facility openings and existing facility fee reviews. Even in these cases, municipal housing, road occupancy fees, schools and others facilities subject to legal calculations, or independent accounting for water-works, hospitals and such, must use their own respective calculation methods. Apart from these, the basic formula to express the concept of usage fees is as follows:

Usage Fee
= Cost price (A) × Beneficiary's burden ratio (B)

Let's examine these elements in detail.
(A) Cost price
The calculation of the cost price follows the full-cost principle. Full cost includes ① running cost (maintenance and operational expenses) and ② initial cost (expenses incurred for facility acquisition), comprising the total. The running cost is the annual total of staff wages, utility bills, maintenance and repair costs, contract expenses, and other facility-related costs. If an existing facility, actual figures are used; for new facilities, estimated figures are calculated. Among these, personnel costs can be complex. Simply collecting the salary paid annually can capture the reality on the ground, but large fluctuations in total salary due to annual changes can affect the basis for calculating usage fees. Therefore, many local governments calculate a standard amount based on staffing levels. Even when calculating a standard amount, methods that reflect the actual situation, such as average salary by occupation and grade, must be considered.

The initial cost is the depreciation expense for fixed assets like buildings and equipment, calculated according to their usage period and totaled for one year. For land costs, one might consider the equivalent amount for one year's land rent, but many examples exclude this from the initial cost, as it can be repurposed for other facilities even if no longer in use.

In the method described above, we tally the full cost for one year and set individual unit prices. A calculation example based on area standards, such as a rented conference room, is as follows:

① Price per square meter per hour
= Facility cost (annual) ÷ Floor area (m²) ÷ Available hours per year

② Price per room per hour
= ① × Area used: For charges like public pool usage fees, which cannot be allocated by area, a method based on the number of users can be considered.

The specific calculation is as follows:
Cost per person
= Facility cost (annual) ÷ Gross floor area × Area used ÷ Annual number of users (capacity)

(B) Beneficiary Burden Ratio
If municipalities can cover all administrative services through fees, private entities most likely can undertake similar services. However, many services indispensable to residents' lives cannot be provided by private entities due to their public nature or profitability issues. Therefore, it is necessary to provide these services using not only fees but also taxes as funding. This ratio between fees, taxes, and other funds is referred to as the beneficiary burden ratio, which must be set for each facility according to the characteristics of the facility and local conditions.

The beneficiary burden ratio is considered based on two classifications. One is classification by necessity, which considers whether the local government should provide the service or not to residents. For essential services (high necessity), the publicly funded proportion is increased; for optional services (low necessity), the fee proportion is increased. The other is classification by marketability, which considers whether similar services are available privately. Services with low marketability and high public benefit are covered with a higher publicly funded proportion, while those with high marketability and available privately have a higher fee proportion.

These two considerations are taken as vertical and horizontal axes, and arbitrary criteria are set from 0 to 100 percent. The facility is then classified and the beneficiary burden ratio set accordingly. For instance, a service that is indispensable to daily life (high necessity) but cannot be provided privately (low marketability) may have a zero percent beneficiary burden ratio. Conversely, a service chosen by residents to improve their lives (low necessity) and available privately (high marketability) may have a 100 percent beneficiary burden ratio. The illustration is as follows:

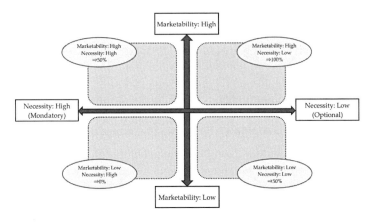

Figure 9-1. Concept of the Beneficiary's Burden Ratio (Created by the author)

Methods of Calculating Administrative Fees

The basic approach to administrative fee calculation is the same for usage charges. Fees are calculated by multiplying the beneficiary burden ratio by the fee cost, which represents the portion of the cost of receiving public services that should be borne by the beneficiary. It also excludes fees whose calculation methods are determined by various laws. In this case, the fee cost includes various expenses, such as personnel costs and system usage fees, and the processing time per case is also taken into account for the calculation.

Profit and Loss Statement by Facility

So far we have examined fee structure and handling charges. The creation of forms from scratch to calculate the actual cost of these charges can be labor intensive, so utilizing the existing New Local Government Accounting System is recommended. This system is used by nearly all municipalities across the country to prepare such financial documents as balance sheets and profit and loss statements in a unified format. Minor adjustments can be made to the profit and loss statements.

This statement calculates the net administrative cost by subtracting the reciprocal usage fees and handling charges from various expenses related to administrative services. From the municipality's overall profit and loss statement, the relevant expenses and revenue related to the specific facility are extracted. However, since this solely calculates the usage fees, incidental costs and revenue are excluded, with a focus only on regular expenses and income.

We can categorize the expenses as follows.

1. Costs Related to Personnel: As previously discussed in the context of fee cost, calculate the labour costs based on standard staffing levels and working hours at the facility, including related expenses such as mutual aid fees. Additionally, calculate the amount to be borne in the fiscal year for future retirement benefits and bonuses for the following year, and apportion these expenses to each facility.

2. Costs Related to Goods: This includes fees for contracted services, maintenance and repair costs, and depreciation expenses. For contract fees paid to the designated administrator, allocate fees such as labour costs to the appropriate accounts based on the breakdown provided. Extract and aggregate the depreciation expenses from the fixed asset ledger for buildings, construction, and goods related to the facility. Naturally, ensure there are no omissions in asset recording. If anything is unrecorded or recorded improperly, adjust the fixed asset ledger accordingly.

3. Transfer Expenditure-Type Costs: Aggregate the expenses such as subsidies and taxes paid to external organizations.

4. Other Costs: Aggregate all other expenses, for example, interest payments on bonds borrowed to construct a facility, that do not fall into categories 1 to 3.

To aggregate expenses related to the facility, the utilization of data from the financial system regarding expenditures will help prevent omissions. Be mindful to avoid overlooking costs related to the facility based on budget codes or project codes. Recently, for administrative efficiency, there may be bulk payments for expenses like water and electricity. In such cases, you need to inquire with the relevant department to understand the expenses for each facility.

Furthermore, with the increase in multi-purpose complex facilities in recent years, it is necessary to rationally allocate costs such as depreciation and utilities based on the floor area or the number of users.

Calculating the cost of fees provides basic information; however, creating a detailed profit

【Operating Expenses】 Unit: Yen

Category		Fiscal Year X
Costs Related to Personnel	(1) Personnel Expenses	25,000,000
	(2) Retirement Allowance Provision Amount	1,000,000
	(3) Bonus Allowance Provision Amount	50,000
	Subtotal	26,050,000
Costs Related to Goods	(1) Property Expenses	80,000,000
	(2) Maintenance and Repair Expenses	2,000,000
	(3) Depreciation	50,000,000
	Subtotal	132,000,000
Transfer Expenditure-Type Costs	(1) Social Security Benefits	
	(2) Grants, etc.	100,000
	(3) Expenditure to Other Accounts	
	(4) Other Transfer Expenses	500,000
	Subtotal	600,000
Other Costs	(1) Interest Payments	10,000
	(2) Provision for Uncollectable Amounts	
	(3) Others	100,000
	Subtotal	110,000
Total Regular Administrative Costs (a)		158,760,000

【Operating Revenue】

Usage Fees & Handling Charges		5,000,000
Others		
Total Regular Revenues (b)		5,000,000

Net Regular Administrative Cost ① (a - b)		153,760,000

【Indicator】

Number of Users (people)		100,000
Cost per Unit	Net Regular Administrative Cost ÷ Number of Users (people)	1,538
Cost per Citizen		
Beneficiary Burden Rate (%)		3.15%

Figure 9-2. Example of Facility-Specific Administrative Costs (Created by the author)

and loss statement by facility would offer a deeper understanding of its current situation. Include revenue as well, such as vending machine fees and other income, based on actual revenue data. In general, subsidies from the national or prefectural governments are excluded, and depending on the situation, recurring subsidies may be included, but subsidies related to asset acquisition must be excluded.

With the aggregation of expenses and revenues, the profit and loss statement by facility, as shown in Figure 9-2, is completed, and the administrative cost by facility can be utilized to examine whether

1. The beneficiary burden rate for the relevant facility is not too low.

2. There are no disparities in usage fees among similar facilities such as community centers.

3. Cost reduction is achieved as initially expected with a designated administrator in place.

If there are no similar facilities in your municipality, you may consider collaborating with neighboring municipalities for comparison's sake. In that case, it is essential to negotiate and unify the accounting standards for various expenses such as labour costs.

Reduction and Exemption Measures

Local governments invariably have these reduction and exemption measures in place for facilities they own. I believe these provisions are often applied mainly to the disabled and elderly based on local ordinances and regulations. Even if the calculation methods for usage fees and handling fees have been transparent so far, it is all for naught if the reduction and exemption provisions are applied arbitrarily. Many cases can be found where these provisions are vaguely expressed and no revisions made for several years. There are also instances where the reduction rate was set by the person in charge at the time, with the basis for that rate not shown and continuing to this day with no handover of the rationale to the current person in charge.

It is necessary to prevent these situations by continually reviewing and revising, if necessary, the contents of the reduction and exemption provisions. It is also essential to carefully examine individual applications to ensure compliance with the provisions, whether undue consideration is being given to specific groups, and to revisit the application in conjunction with opportunities to review the usage fees.

Conclusion

In an era of population decline, the number of people using public facilities will inevitably decrease, leading to a natural reduction in usage fees. Tax revenues will also fall, and we must recognize the limits to maintaining the current facilities in the same way going forward. The reconsideration of usage and handling fees will be unavoidable if administrative services are to be maintained as before. However, it will be difficult for residents to accept increases in these fees.

I believe there are three key points to revising facility handling and usage fees. The first is "transparency." It is obvious to disclose the basis for calculating usage fees, but it is equally important to clarify the basis for applying reduction and exemption measures while considering fairness. The second point is "regular reviews." Even if the situation and actual use of the facility change, usage fees should be reflected after regularly checking whether they have been stagnant for a long time, or whether there is waste in the cost of service providers. However, drastic price increases should be avoided, and consideration given to gradual increases through transitional measures. The third point is "sustainability." Residents may resist cutting administrative services, but we must examine whether the facilities are really necessary, whether alternative facilities can be prepared, or if they can be shared with neighboring local governments. Consolidation and multi-facility integration are progressing everywhere, but there are examples in advanced local governments of upgrading facilities by introducing private-sector vitality through PFI and other methods, thereby increasing user numbers and residents' satisfaction. Lastly, to examine the realignment of facilities, I would like to emphasize that utilizing public accounting information, which is prepared in principle by all local governments, is the most efficient approach, and with that I conclude this chapter.

References

※Ichinomiya City, Aichi Prefecture, "Basic Policy on the Review of Usage Fees and Handling Fees" (August, Reiwa 1)

※Narashino City, Chiba Prefecture, "Narashino City Standard for Calculating Unit Prices of Usage Fees, Handling Fees, Etc. (revised edition)" (January, Heisei 31)

Chapter 10

Comprehensive Management Plan for Public Facilities

Tax Accountant: Ryota Hirose

Introduction

Since August 2022, a study group on The Future of Local Government Accounting has been conducted at the Ministry of Internal Affairs and Communications. In About the Meeting of the Study Group on the Future of Local Government Accounting (1st Time), despite the theme of local public accounting, the following items related to the fixed asset ledger were listed as topics for discussion (excerpted from the topics below).

(1) Examination of additional methods for utilizing local public accounting information
• Utilization of the fixed asset ledger (public facility management, etc.)

(2) Verification and improvement of unified standards
• Refinement of the fixed asset ledger (improving accuracy, linking with facilities)
• Coordination between the fixed asset ledger and other ledgers (public property ledger, etc.)

This chapter will introduce the history of the Comprehensive Management Plan for Public Facilities and its collaboration with local public accounting and fixed asset ledgers, as well as future application methods for the fixed asset ledger in public facility management as discussed in the study group.

Historical Public Facility Management (Comprehensive Management Plan for Public Facilities)

Historical public facility management (Comprehensive Management Plan for Public Facilities) is shown in Table 10-1. The author was deeply shocked by the collapse of the Sasago Tunnel in 2012; unlike damage from an earthquake, this was a human-made disaster caused by decaying infrastructure. Clearly there is a need for public facility management by local public entities (municipalities) to have a maximum impact on aging public facilities within the framework of limited financial resources.

In 2013, the Ministry of Land, Infrastructure, Transport, and Tourism compiled the Basic Plan for Infrastructure Longevity as an initiative for measures to combat aging infrastructure. Moving forward, based on this plan it was decided to improve the safety of all national infrastructure while ensuring efficient maintenance and management by formulating action plans at the national and local government levels. The outline of this plan is as fol-

Table 10-1. Previous Public Facility Management (Comprehensive Management Plan for Public Facilities)

F/Y	Public Facility Management (Comprehensive Management Plan for Public Facilities)
2013	Formulation of the national "Infrastructure Longevity Basic Plan."
2014	Request to formulate the "Comprehensive Management Plan for Public Facilities" (Notification by the Minister of Internal Affairs).
	Formulation of guidelines (Notification by the Director of Financial Inspection, Local Finance Bureau, Ministry of Internal Affairs).
	Establishment of special local tax measures for expenses required to create the Comprehensive Management Plan for Public Facilities (until 2016).
2016	Issuance of "Further Promotion of Public Facility Management" (Finance Inspection Division Office Communication)※ Notification through the publication of case studies, etc. ≪ Formulation deadline for the Comprehensive Management Plan (reform schedule) ≫
2017	Revision of the "Guidelines for Formulating the Comprehensive Management Plan for Public Facilities" (Notification by the Director of the Finance Inspection Division).
2018	Issuance of "Further Promotion of Proper Management of Public Facilities" (Finance Inspection Division Office Communication). ※ Announcement of ideas for revising the comprehensive management plan.
2020	Issuance of "Points to Note for Revising the Comprehensive Management Plan for Public Facilities until Fiscal 2021" (Finance Inspection Division Office Communication).
2022	Formulation deadline for the Individual Facility Plan (reform schedule).
2023	Revision deadline for the Comprehensive Management Plan for Public Facilities (reform schedule).

lows:

- Building a maintenance cycle centered on individual facility longevity plans.
- Reducing and leveling the total costs through the execution of the maintenance cycle and the construction of systems.
- Developing new technologies and nurturing the maintenance industry through industry, academia, and government collaboration.

In 2014, the Ministry of Internal Affairs and Communications compiled the Guidelines for Formulating Comprehensive Public Facility Management Plans. Each local government was required to undertake the formulation of a comprehensive management plan for public facilities. Aimed at comprehensively and systematically managing public facilities, the plan sets out the basic policies for the current status of owned facilities and overall facility management. The outline of promoting aging infrastructure countermeasures based on the comprehensive management plan is as follows.

(1) Management of Public Facilities
• Promotion of aging infrastructure countermeasures from a long-term perspective
• Implementation of proper maintenance, repair, and management
• Reduction and leveling of total costs
• Continuous review and enhancement of the plan

(2) Town Planning
• Utilization of PPP/PFI
• Consideration with a view to future town development
• Sharing information and awareness of the current situation with the assembly and residents

(3) National Resilience
• Planned inspections and diagnoses
• Accumulation of records of repairs and renewals
• Ensuring the safety of public facilities
• Promotion of seismic resistance

Also, based on the comprehensive management plan, the formulation of individual facility plans has been requested by each administrative agency in charge of the facilities. To be formulated by 2022, individual facility plans will specify the specific response policies for individual facilities based on inspections and diagnoses, prioritizing measures for maintenance and renewal, including the content and timing of measures, and the cost of these measures.

In 2020, the Ministry of Internal Affairs and Communications issued Points to Note Regarding the Revision of the Comprehensive Management Plan for Public Facilities, etc. for 2021, requesting that local governments review the comprehensive management plan by 2021 based on individual facility plans.

History Related to Fixed Asset Ledgers

In private companies, the fixed asset ledger is essential for asset information management, but local governments are behind in its preparation. The Ministry of Internal Affairs and Communications established the Working Subcommittee on the Development of Fixed Asset Ledgers in Local Public Entities (Subcommittee) under the research meeting, and practical discussions were conducted. In 2014, the Working Subcommittee Report on the

Development of Fixed Asset Ledgers in Local Public Entities (Subcommittee Report) was published.

In 2014, the Ministry of Internal Affairs and Communications set unified standards for preparing financial statements, assuming the development of fixed asset ledgers and the introduction of double-entry bookkeeping, in the Research Report on the Promotion of the New Local Government Accounting System. As a result, all local governments have proceeded to develop fixed asset ledgers. The procedure manual presented at this time for the development of fixed asset ledgers is the Guide for Asset Valuation and Fixed Asset Ledger Development (Ledger Guide). The Ledger Guide has now been integrated with other manuals to form the Unified Standard Local Government Accounting Manual.

The fixed asset ledger is defined in both the Subcommittee Report and the Ledger Guide as follows.

(1) Subcommittee Report
The fixed asset ledger is "an auxiliary book used for managing fixed assets, recording acquisition costs, elements necessary for depreciation calculation, depreciation amount, accumulated depreciation, balance after depreciation, and records related to disposal or sale. Fixed asset ledgers can be divided into land ledgers, building ledgers, machinery ledgers, equipment ledgers, etc." (Taken from the Third Edition Accounting Dictionary, edited by Kobe University Accounting Research Room.)

(2) Ledger Guide
A fixed asset ledger is a book for managing fixed assets from acquisition to disposal, encompassing all fixed assets (roads, parks, schools, community centers, etc.), including acquisition costs, and service life. Fixed assets differ from expenses consumed in one year and are used in administrative services over the long term, making accounting value management necessary.

The Subcommittee Report describes the issues related to how the fixed asset ledger is organized, while the Ledger Guide documents the methods for utilizing the fixed asset ledger for public facility management.

(1) Subcommittee Report
The Subcommittee Report highlights issues concerning the organization of the fixed asset ledger. These issues include the frequent cases of unknown acquisition costs and funding

sources, the need for specialized knowledge in asset evaluation, significant human and financial burdens, hesitation in organizing the ledger due to unclear cost-effectiveness, difficulty in understanding the objections to organization or utility value, and struggles with intra-agency coordination, among others. As reference material in the same report, the following matters have been raised over these issues.

① Entities with the ledger
• Many cases have unknown acquisition costs and funding sources, requiring time for the identification, reconciliation, and evaluation of numerous assets.
• Specialized and extensive knowledge is demanded for asset evaluation.
• For infrastructure assets such as roads, previously excluded from traditional property management systems, a substantial amount of work and time is required for investigation.
• There are difficulties in distinguishing capital expenditures and repair costs, categorizing business and infrastructure assets, and determining service life.
• The annual management (update) workload is immense.
• Management (updates) has been challenging due to staff transfers.
• Even though outsourced, annual management expenses pose financial burdens.
• Omissions in ledger registration are discovered after having been organized, leading to reinvestigation.

② Entities under development or Entities with no ledger
• Time is required for identifying, reconciling, and evaluating assets.
• Especially for infrastructure assets such as roads, many cases have unknown acquisition costs that demand extensive valuation work.
• Human and financial burdens are too large to organize, and there is no clear plan.
• Hesitation to undertake the organization of the fixed asset ledger without clear benefits.
• Difficulty in gaining intra-agency understanding of the significance and utility value of ledger organization, and struggling with coordination.
• Although the need is understood, other concurrent duties and staff shortages prevent initiation.
• Lack of staff with specialized knowledge.
• Differences in ledger organization among pre-merged entities require extensive time and effort to consolidate.

(2) Ledger Guide
Under the current system, local public bodies are required to maintain various ledgers such

as the public property ledger mandated by the Local Autonomy Law (Law No. 67 of 1947), and those like road ledgers based on individual laws. Unlike fixed asset ledgers, these ledgers focus mainly on the quantitative aspects of property operation management and current status assessment, without presupposing an understanding of asset value.

Furthermore, although these ledgers are individually maintained, a comprehensive fixed asset ledger covering all fixed assets is not required. In the future, it will be essential to show information related to the fair burden between future and present generations, and segmented financial information by facility and project, and to utilize this information for individual administrative evaluation, budget formation, countermeasures against aging public facilities, and asset management.

Use of these ledgers will also promote the participation of private operators in PPP/PFI projects. Moreover, connecting fixed asset ledger utilization through comprehensive and planned management of public facilities and a refined basic policy will help facilitate maintenance, repair, and renewal.

The purpose is not just to organize the fixed asset ledger, but also to advance its organization with post-organization use in mind. Although there are many distinctions in purpose and structure between the existing various ledgers and the fixed asset ledger, integrated management is an efficient method of asset management. Data can be retrieved freely from the existing ledgers, and a unified fixed asset ledger can be organized with a view to the future.

Especially for ledgers such as public property ledgers, primarily aimed at property operation management, there is considerable overlap with the fixed asset ledger. To maintain their consistency and efficient management, it is desirable, for example, to share and link asset numbers.

The Future of Public Facility Management

In considering the future of public facility management, reference can be made to the materials publicly disclosed by the study group on The Future of Local Government Accounting by the Ministry of Internal Affairs and Communications. The status of "development" and "utilization" of local government accounting is described in How to Proceed with the Utilization of Local Government Accounting in the Future (October 19, 2022, Ministry of Internal Affairs and Communications, Local Finance Bureau, Finance Division). Development has been completed by almost all local governments, but utilization has hardly progressed. The utilization of financial documents based on "uniform standards" has exceeded 50 percent with 989 entities (55.3%), according to a survey in fiscal 2021. On the other hand, the expected utilization for "comprehensive public facility management planning or individual facility planning" is 408 entities (22.8%), while "materials for reconsidering public facilities" is limited to 61 entities (3.4%). Despite the progress in analysis, utilization in such areas as public facility management remains low.

Several hypotheses exist as to why utilization has not progressed. For example, while information (asset prices, aging conditions, etc.) listed in financial documents and fixed asset ledgers is utilized, this information is not referred to "only" in those records; other legally mandated asset ledgers are also referenced. One hypothesis question whether it is recognized as "utilizing" local government accounting. Another theory suggests that analyses of macro-based aging conditions are conducted in public facility management, but considerations regarding total costs for aggregation/integration and aging infrastructure renewal over the medium to long term are not viewed as options.

In the breakdown analysis of financial documents, there are tangible fixed assets and accumulated depreciation. By analyzing these figures, beneficial data for promoting specific measures for proper management of public facilities (renewal, consolidation/abolition, longevity, etc.) can be obtained, such as explaining to the council and promoting residents' understanding. For example, analyzing by facility type (schools, libraries, government buildings, etc.) allows for objective explanations based on comparisons within the same type of facility and judging the priority of aging infrastructure countermeasures. Analyzing merged municipalities by former municipal areas makes it possible to determine the areas with many aging facilities and to consider the proper placement of facilities in all areas, including the relevant areas. By focusing on the ratio of accumulated depreciation to the amount of tangible fixed assets (acquisition price, etc.), it is possible to grasp the age of the assets owned.

In segment analysis, it is essential to utilize local government accounting information in public facility management. As a utilization strategy for public facility management, it is expected that such facility-specific segment analyses as creating financial documents for each facility and performing cost analysis will be actively used in asset management, such as promoting the progress and improvement of the overall management plan for public facilities. Aging countermeasures for public facilities, including consolidation/complexity, longevity, and decarbonization, are urgent issues for local governments that highlight the need to conduct facility-specific segment analyses. In the Unified Standard Local Government Accounting Manual, examples of "procedures for creating segment-specific financial documents" are provided, but the details are described for individual cost allocation methods when creating profit and loss statements, while lifecycle cost analysis is limited to case introductions. Lifecycle cost (LCC) in public facility management considers the total cost of public facilities and infrastructure, including construction costs (design, construction, construction supervision, etc.), operating costs (utilities), maintenance costs (maintenance, repair, etc.), and demolition/disposal costs (demolition, disposal, etc.).

Given that aging facility countermeasures are an urgent issue, it is conceivable to first proceed with a facility-specific segment analysis. During this process, medium-term maintenance and management expenses, major renovations, and lifecycle cost-inclusive analysis methods should be outlined, with the expectation of further discussions from professional viewpoints and local government needs surveys. A joint project between the Ministry of Internal Affairs and Communications and the Local Public Finance Corporation dispatches advisors according to the situation and requests of the organization. This system aims to strengthen the management and financial management of local public entities and improve the quality of their fiscal management. Although the system used to mainly dispatch advisors to public enterprises, recently it has become possible to dispatch advisors to help develop and utilize local government accounting as well as review and implement (public facility management) comprehensive public facility management plans, and utilization examples have emerged.

Gradual Utilization of the Fixed Asset Ledger in Public Facility Management

In the future, it is anticipated that municipalities will gradually utilize the fixed asset ledger for public facility management. Currently, almost all municipalities utilize the ledger in the following cases:

- Metric analysis (regularly calculating and reporting the tangible fixed assets depreciation rate to the prefecture and national government)
- Revising items in the comprehensive management plan (including trends in the tangible fixed assets depreciation rate)

The tangible fixed assets depreciation rate is an index that calculates the proportion of the accumulated depreciation amount (numerator) to the acquisition cost of the depreciated asset (denominator) among tangible fixed assets in order to comprehensively understand how far the asset has surpassed its service life. This index is used as one of the local government accounting financial indicators. For example, in Machida City, Tokyo, the tangible fixed assets depreciation rate is utilized in public facility management to calculate the depreciation rate for each type of facility. The author has also calculated the facility type-specific tangible fixed assets depreciation rate when revising the comprehensive management plan of municipalities.

Furthermore, cases where the national government (Ministry of Internal Affairs and Communications) expects municipalities to utilize the tangible fixed assets depreciation rate at an early stage include:

• Coordination with local government accounting financial statements (tangible fixed assets, accumulated depreciation)
• Creation of facility-specific profit and loss statements

Moreover, the national government actively expects each municipality to work on the following items in the medium term (contributing to the resolution of financial issues, thus utilizing the tangible fixed assets depreciation rate in municipal management):

• Lifecycle cost analysis
• Utilization of facility-specific profit and loss statements in budgeting

There is an initiative in Hamamatsu City, Shizuoka Prefecture, that provides an example of an advanced municipality (consideration of facility construction including lifecycle costs). In Hamamatsu, the discussion of new facility construction in budgeting centered on initial costs, and the discussion that included future maintenance and renewal costs (lifecycle costs) was not always sufficient. As a result, facility-specific profit and loss statements (estimates) are now used as review materials in budgeting for new construction facilities, and comprehensive discussions are held incorporating lifecycle costs, such as maintenance costs for facilities, in the budgeting.

Updating the fixed asset ledger is essential, regardless of its stage of utilization, not just as a subsidiary ledger for local government accounting but also for public facility management. As an advisor for the Management and Financial Management Business of Local Public Entities (Public Accounting and Public Facility Relations) of the Ministry of Internal Affairs and Communications, the author has been supporting the creation of a standard model and uniform standard financial statements during the introduction of fixed asset ledgers, or "individual facility plans," along with supporting the revision of the Comprehensive Management Plan for Public Facilities. (Note: These plans include buildings and infrastructure assets such as roads and rivers, but this chapter is limited to buildings.)

The author has also been involved in supporting the development of the fixed asset ledger for local public entity public accounting, and is currently engaged in updating the support for public accounting fixed asset ledgers through the creation of local government accounting financial statements. Updating of the fixed asset ledger varies among local public entities, with some using an all-agency system, and others by local government accounting and facility-related personnel. It has been almost ten years since the Ministry of Internal Affairs and Communications' Working Group Report on the Development of Fixed Asset Ledgers in Local Public Entities (2014), but the original goal of "utilizing asset information in administrative management" has not been achieved. It is presumed that the voice of local government has not changed from the time of the report (10 years ago) to the present day.

Since the accuracy of the fixed asset ledger varies from municipality to municipality, and updating is left to the capacity of each municipality, comparability between municipalities cannot be ensured. Although a local government's fixed asset ledger is published in principle, it seems that each municipality only discloses the minimum necessary information about the fixed asset ledger. It is felt that more efforts such as adding explanations to make the ledger easier for residents to understand are necessary. Not only for local government accounting but also for the sake of public facility management, perhaps this task could be carried out by professionals of a certain level or higher. In the future, the Ministry of Internal Affairs and Communications should hold a Working Group on Updating Fixed Asset Ledgers in Local Public Entities (provisional name), and set deadlines for each local public entity to update their fixed asset ledger to the desired form (contributing to public facility management comparable with other local public entities).

References

※Ministry of Internal Affairs and Communications, "Study Group on the Future Direction of Local Government Accounting" (scheduled for 2022-2023)

※Yuji Nemoto "Decaying Infrastructure: Another Looming Crisis," Nihon Keizai Shimbun Publishing (2011)

※Ministry of Land, Infrastructure, Transport and Tourism website, "Infrastructure Longevity Basic Plan" (2013) [https://www.mlit.go.jp/sogoseisaku/sosei_point_mn_000010.html]

※Ministry of Internal Affairs and Communications website, "Guidelines for the Formulation of a Comprehensive Management Plan for Public Facilities, Etc." (2014) [https://www.soumu.go.jp/main_content/000287574.pdf]

※Ministry of Internal Affairs and Communications website, Overview of the "Guidelines for the Formulation of a Comprehensive Management Plan for Public Facilities, Etc." (2014) [https://www.soumu.go.jp/main_content/000287575.pdf]

※Ministry of Internal Affairs and Communications, "Working Group Report on the Development of Fixed Asset Ledgers in Local Public Entities" (2014)

※Ministry of Internal Affairs and Communications, "Local Government Accounting Manual According to Uniform Standards" (revised August 2019)

※Building Maintenance Center, "Building Lifecycle Costs, 2nd edition" (2019)

Chapter 11

Management of Public Enterprises

(Water Supply Services)

Nihon Suido Consultants Co.,Ltd. - Akihisa Hirata

Introduction

In this chapter I will discuss the management of public enterprises, focusing particularly on the water supply services. In September 2022, the reorganization of the Ministry of Health, Labour, and Welfare was announced, bringing to the spotlight the transfer of water administration to the Ministry of Land, Infrastructure, Transport, and Tourism and the Ministry of the Environment. Not only that, the role of water supply as a lifeline has been emphasized in the event of large-scale natural disasters, and although not a natural disaster, the importance of maintaining and managing aged and deteriorated facilities was again recognized in the water pipeline bridge accident in Wakayama City in October of 2021. Furthermore, with the amendment to the Water Supply Act in December 2018, allowing the establishment of a concession system by private operators to promote public-private collaboration, various debates were held on the "privatization of the water supply services," a matter still fresh in our memory.

In this context we will examine the positioning of public enterprises, recent national policies, and other relevant issues, present the environment surrounding the water supply services and current challenges, and discuss responses from a resource (people, things, and money) management perspective.

What Are Public Enterprises, Local Public Enterprises, and Water Supply Services?

Public enterprises are businesses operated by local governments, with special accounts set up based on Article 6 of the Local Finance Act; they do not have their own legal personality and belong to local governments. This is stipulated in Article 46 of the Enforcement Order of the Local Finance Act and includes forms subject to Article 2 of the Local Public Enterprise Act, with those subject to the Local Public Enterprise Act referred to as local public enterprises. Local public enterprises are managed by prefectures and municipalities, without a legal personality, and operate on an independent accounting basis, separate from the general account (administrative budget).

Also, special accounts are often used by public enterprises to manage sewage and small water supply services, which are not required to apply the provisions of the Local Public Enterprise Act. However, to provide stable and sustainable services, an accurate understanding of management information, demonstration of economic efficiency, and a comparison of management conditions among companies are necessary. Based on this thinking, the Ministry of Internal Affairs and Communications promotes the application of the Local Public Enterprise Act and the adoption of public enterprise accounting.

Table 11-1. Excerpts from the Local Finance Act, Local Finance Act Enforcement Order, and Local Public Enterprise Act

【Local Finance Act】
(Public Enterprise Management)
Article 6: For public enterprises designated by Cabinet Order, their management shall be carried out by establishing a special account, and the expenses shall be covered by the income associated with the management of the enterprise, excluding expenses deemed inappropriate due to their nature, and expenses that are objectively difficult to cover solely by the income associated with management. However, in case of a disaster or other special circumstances, and upon approval by the assembly, public enterprises may be funded by revenue transferred from the general account or other special accounts.

【Local Finance Act Enforcement Order】
(Public Enterprise)
Article 46: Public enterprises designated by Article 6 of the Law shall be the businesses listed below.
1. Water Supply Services, 2. Industrial Water Supply Services, 3. Transportation Business, 4. Electric Power Business, 5. Gas Business, 6. Small Water Supply Services, 7. Harbor Improvement Business (limited to land reclamation and cargo handling equipment, shelters, warehouses, lumber yards, and ships for assisting ship berthing), 8. Hospital Business, 9. Market Business, 10. Slaughterhouse Business, 11. Tourist Facility Business, 12. Residential Land Development Business, 13. Public Sewerage Services

【Local Public Enterprise Act】
(Scope of Enterprises Subject to this Law)
Article 2: This law applies to the businesses managed by local public entities listed below (including related businesses; hereinafter referred to as "local public enterprises").
1. Water Supply Services (excluding small water supply services), 2. Industrial Water Supply Services, 3. Rail Business, 4. Motor Vehicle Transport Business, 5. Railway Business, 6. Electric Power Business, 7. Gas Business

Source: e-GOV Legal Search https://elaws.e-gov.go.jp/

Focusing on the water supply services, the Local Public Enterprise Act applies to local public enterprises, and the method of conducting business is defined in the Water Supply Act. Article 1 of the Water Supply Act states, "The purpose of this law is to properly and reasonably control the installation and management of waterworks, to enhance the water infrastructure, to ensure the supply of clean, abundant, and low-cost water, thereby contributing to the improvement of public health and living environment." It clearly states that the Water Supply Act governs the establishment and management of facilities, emphasizing cleanliness, abundance, and low cost as the three main principles. In addition, when considering the water supply services from the perspective of public facility management, as shown in the table below, public facilities can be classified into public facilities, official facilities, and public welfare facilities, among others, as well as divided into artificial structures and natural terrains.

Furthermore, from the perspective of facility management, water supply services are governed by business law (Water Supply Act), and sewerage services are regulated by public property management law (Sewerage Act). Public property management law consists of standards for the administration to manage public facilities and conditions imposed on facility users (exercise of public authority), while business law embodies the conditions for application and administration approval when a business operator provides public/welfare services (guaranteeing stable services).

Often handled organizationally as one in water and sewerage departments, the positioning of water and sewerage facilities and the laws governing their management differ, so caution is required.

Table 11-2. Classification of Public Facilities

	Public Facility		Government Facility	Public Welfare Facility	Others
Artificial	Sewerage Road Park Harbor, etc.	Water Supply Railway, etc.	Government OfficeDormitory, etc.	Education Facility Healthcare Facility Waste Treatment Facility Public Housing, etc.	Telecommunication Facility Heat Supply Facility, etc.
Natural	River Coast, etc.	-	-	-	-
	Public Property Management Law	Each Respective Business Law	-	-	Each Respective Business Law

Recent National Policies concerning Water Supply Services

Water supply services have been described as operating based on the Water Supply Act, but in this section, I will explain the recent national policies concerning the amendment to the Water Supply Act and the transfer of water supply administration.

First, regarding the amendment to the Water Supply Act, a bill to amend a portion of the Water Supply Act to enhance the foundation of water supply was enacted in December 2018, and enforced on October 1, 2019. The amended Water Supply Act changes the purpose of the law from "planned development of water supply" to "strengthening the foundation of the water supply." It also prescribes the promotion of wide-area collaboration, appropriate asset management, public-private collaboration, and improvement of the designated water supply equipment construction business system. Here I will focus on the "promotion of public-private collaboration."

As a comprehensive government effort amid the nation's population decline, various forms of public-private collaboration are being considered to ensure stable water supply services management and efficient development and management in accordance with local circumstances. Public-private collaboration is seen as an endeavor aimed ensuring the sustainability of water supply services and improving public service quality. Local public bodies responsible for water supply services and water supply for water supply services must from a long-term perspective, depending on their circumstances, collaborate with private companies able to offer excellent technology, business know-how and familiarity with local conditions. This requirement is positioned as one of the effective measures for strengthening the foundation of the water supply services.

Based on the amended Water Supply Act, the Basic Policy for Strengthening the Foundation of Water Supply, formulated in September 2019, also regards public-private collaboration as "one of the effective options for strengthening the foundation of water supply." The policy states, "It is important to clarify the purpose of utilizing public-private collaboration and implement appropriate forms of collaboration according to regional realities." There are various forms of public-private collaboration in water supply services and water supply for water supply services, including the commissioning of individual tasks, the commissioning of comprehensive tasks, third-party commissioning involving legal responsibility under the Water Supply Act, and the use of DBO (Note 1) and PFI (Note 2). In addition, the "concession system" based on the Act on Promotion of Private Finance Initiative was made feasible by strengthening public involvement while maintaining the position of local governments as water supply operators, and by allowing private operators to manage water supply facilities with the permission of the Minister of Health, Labour and Welfare.

Next, as part of the Ministry of Health, Labour and Welfare's efforts to enhance its ability to respond to infectious diseases, the policy to transfer water supply administration was announced in September 2022. Specifically, water supply development and management administration are expected to be centrally managed by the Ministry of Land, Infrastructure, Transport and Tourism, and will likely be operated in conjunction with sewerage administration at the Water Management and Land Conservation Bureau. The formulation of water quality and other standards is expected to be managed by the Ministry of the Environment and transferred to the Water and Air Environment Bureau. The transfer is aimed for April 2024.

Looking back briefly, drinking water hygiene administration was the responsibility of the Ministry of Health and Welfare, and technical matters related to construction were under the jurisdiction of the Ministry of Construction. In January 1957, the Cabinet decided to divide water supply administration into three parts (water supply: Ministry of Health and Welfare, sewerage: Ministry of Construction, and industrial water supply: Ministry of International Trade and Industry), and since then, water supply administration has been consistently handled by the Ministry of Health, Labour and Welfare (formerly the Ministry of Health and Welfare). This transfer of water supply administration was the first change in the system in about 70 years, and there is hope that the technical capabilities of the Ministry of Land, Infrastructure, Transport and Tourism (implementation of directly managed projects by civil engineers), including groundwater and rainwater use, and sewage treatment water reuse as a water circulation system, will address the problems and challenges faced by water supply services.

Changes in the Environment Surrounding Water Supply Services

Water supply services have achieved a 98.0 percent penetration rate and are transitioning from an era predicated on the expansion of water supply to an era requiring the solidification of existing water supply infrastructure. However, the industry faces the following challenges.

Internal Challenges within the Water Supply Services

① Aging infrastructure
Water supply facilities developed during the period of rapid economic growth up to around 1975 are aging and deteriorating. Water pipelines account for a large part of the nation's water assets, yet suffer over 20,000 incidents of leaks and damages annually. Pipeline renewal is underway, but the renewal rate is stagnating at an average of 0.67 percent nationwide (as of fiscal year 2019). The proportion of pipelines exceeding their statutory service life is increasing year by year (19.1% nationwide average as of fiscal 2019).

② Lag in earthquake resistance measures
According to a fiscal 2020 report by the Ministry of Health, Labour and Welfare, the earthquake resistance rate for water purification facilities is 38.0 percent, for distribution reservoirs 60.8 percent, and for main pipelines 26.8 percent, with an earthquake compatibility rate of 40.7 percent. Given the increasing probability of earthquakes such as the Nankai Trough earthquake, these figures are not particularly high. This indicates a lack of progress in earthquake-proofing the water supply systems, leading to the risk of prolonged water outages in the event of a major earthquake.

③ Numerous small water suppliers with a fragile management base
Water supply services are mainly operated at the municipal level, and many water suppliers are small with a vulnerable management base. Largely affected by the mass retirement of baby boomer employees and staff reductions through administrative rationalization, small water suppliers face the challenges of passing on technology, proper asset management, daily operations, and crisis management. Moreover, in a declining population society under worsening management conditions, there is concern that water services might not continue in the years ahead.

④ Insufficient preparation for systematic renewal
The national scale of water assets exceeds 40 trillion yen. Renewing these water facilities will require enormous time and cost. However, for about one third of water suppliers, the cost of water supply exceeds the supply unit price, and many suppliers cannot secure the necessary funds needed for planned renewals.

External Challenges Surrounding the Water Supply Services

① Decrease in Population and Water Demand:

Japan's population has already shifted from a declining birth rate to an overall population decline. It is estimated that by 2050 the population will fall to around 100 million. According to a report by the Ministry of Health, Labour and Welfare, water demand is also expected to decrease, with water intake estimated to drop by almost 40 percent by 2050 (from about 41 million m3/day in 2000 to about 27 million m3/day in 2050). Given that the water supply industry operates on a fixed cost basis that do not decrease regardless of the water supply amount, a decrease in water supply will directly lead to a reduction in revenue. Considering the shrinking water supply and the need to downsize water facilities, simply maintaining the current size for renewal will lead to inefficiencies, including reduced facility utilization. Restructuring water facilities in light of Japan's population decline is a challenge that all water suppliers will face in the future.

② Various Rising Risks:

As shown in the table below, in addition to the increasing number of major earthquakes and hydrological disasters, risks to the water supply services are rising due to factors such as water source contamination (degradation of raw water quality) and decreased water safety in water resource development facilities like dams (more vulnerable to drought due to climate change). Responses to these risks are necessary.

Table 11-3. Recent Damage to Water Supplies Caused by Natural Disasters

	Disaster Name	Date of Occurrence	Number of Water Outages	Duration of Water Outage
Major damage caused by earthquakes	Great Hanshin-Awaji Earthquake	Jan 17, 1995	Approx. 1.3 million households	Approx. 3 months
	Niigata Prefecture Chuetsu Earthquake	Oct 23, 2004	Approx. 130,000 households	*Approx. 1 month
	Niigata Prefecture Chuetsu Offshore Earthquake	July 16, 2007	Approx. 59,000 households	20 days
	Iwate-Miyagi Inland Earthquake	June 14, 2008	Approx. 5,600 households	*18 days
	Great East Japan Earthquake	March 11, 2011	Approx. 2.567 million households	*Approx. 5 months
	Nagano Prefecture Kamishiro Fault Earthquake	Nov 22, 2014	Approx. 1.300 households	25 days
	Kumamoto Earthquake	April 14-16, 2016	Approx. 446,000 households	*Approx. 3½ months
	Tottori Prefecture Central Earthquake	Oct 21, 2016	Approx. 16,000 households	4 days

Earthquake in Northern Osaka Prefecture	June 12, 2018	Approx. 94,000 households	2 days
Hokkaido Eastern Iburi Earthquake	Sept 6, 2018	Approx. 68,000 households	*34 days
Fukushima Offshore Earthquake	Feb 13, 2021	Approx. 27,000 households	6 days
Fukushima Offshore Earthquake	March 15, 2022	Approx. 70,000 households	7 days
Main Damage from Heavy Rain, Heavy Snow (Hokuriku Region, Chugoku Shikoku Region)	Jan-Feb 2018	Approx. 36,000 households	12 days
Heavy Rain (Hiroshima Prefecture, Ehime Prefecture, Okayama Prefecture)	July 18	Approx. 263,000 households	38 days
Typhoon No. 21 (Kyoto Prefecture, Osaka Prefecture)	Sept 18	Approx. 16,000 households	12 days
Typhoon No. 24 (Shizuoka Prefecture, Miyazaki Prefecture)	Sept 18	Approx. 20,000 households	19 days
Boso Peninsula Typhoon (Chiba Prefecture, Tokyo, Shizuoka Prefecture)	Sept 19	Approx. 140,000 households	17 days
Eastern Japan Typhoon (Miyagi Prefecture, Fukushima Prefecture, Ibaraki Prefecture, Tochigi Prefecture)	Oct 19	Approx. 168,000 households	33 days
Heavy Rain (Kumamoto Prefecture, Oita Prefecture, Nagano Prefecture, Gifu Prefecture)	July 20	Approx. 38,000 households	56 days
Heavy Snow (Western Japan)	Jan 21	Approx. 16,000 households	8 days
Heavy Rain (Akita Prefecture, Yamagata Prefecture, Niigata Prefecture, Fukui Prefecture)	Aug 22	Approx. 14,000 households	18 days
Typhoon No. 14 (Kumamoto Prefecture, Oita Prefecture, Kagoshima Prefecture)	Sept 22	Approx. 13,000 households	9 days
Typhoon No. 15 (Shizuoka Prefecture)	Sept 22	Approx. 76,000 households	13 days

(The lower group of rows is labelled along the left margin: "Major damage caused by heavy rainfall")

※Excluding areas with collapsed houses, fully evacuated areas, and tsunami-affected areas.
Source: Taken from fiscal 2022 water supply technical manager training materials.

Contemporary Challenges (from the Perspective of Management Resources)

So far, I have outlined the legal positioning of public enterprises, the formation of the water supply services, and recent national policies and environmental conditions surrounding the water supply services. Since the theme of this chapter is the management of public enterprises (water supply services), we will now examine contemporary challenges from the perspective of managing the resources of "people, things, and money." The complicated interrelationship of management resources calls for a comprehensive perspective to fully understand these challenges.

1. Challenges Related to "Things"

In responding to natural disasters, water supply operators, as lifeline providers entrusted with life-sustaining water, must be adaptable to deal with various potential crises. Since the Great Hanshin-Awaji Earthquake in 1995, the importance of earthquake resistance for water facilities has been recognized, and efforts have been made to harden facilities against seismic activity. However, progress in increasing the earthquake resistance of water facilities has been sluggish (requiring proactive capital investments), and concerns have arisen about prolonged water outages in the event of a massive widespread disaster disrupting the procurement of water supply materials. There are also challenges in pre-emptive preparation for wide-area procurement (strengthening people and organizations). Moreover, with the recent impacts of climate change, there is a growing probability of heavy rainfall and subsequent landslides that will require corresponding measures.

On the other hand, performance degradation and questionable reliability due to infrastructure aging pose risks to supply stability. Planned and efficient responses that include downsizing to meet renewal demands for aging infrastructure and deteriorating facilities and balanced distribution of renewal needs have become necessary.

2. Challenges Related to "Money"

Water supply operations are primarily conducted on a self-sufficiency system and adhere to corporate accounting principles. For healthy and stable management of these operations, securing income through appropriate water rates is essential. However, decreasing water demand, the failure to optimize pricing, and other factors risk a situation where revenue from water rates falls short. Consequently, many water supply operators are unable to undertake timely renewals or promote earthquake-resistance measures for aging pipelines, purification plants, and related infrastructure (investment in things). Furthermore, staff reductions as a cost-cutting measure could lead to a situation where the number of personnel required to provide proper water services proves insufficient (securing people).

3. Challenges Related to "People"

The water supply services faces numerous challenges related to people, including a severe staff shortage due to relentless personnel reductions and massive retirement of the baby boomer generation; the increasing number of water users that a single staffer must manage annually (increasing staff workload); and the dearth of experienced personnel (problems in technological inheritance). Circumstances like these can trigger a decline in water service quality, risking the loss of local users' trust, and affecting daily water services, rapid response to accidents, and emergency responses during earthquakes or other disasters.

An immediate and realistic response to such problems might include securing human resources through re-employment or re-engagement, but there is an indispensable need for the fundamental assurance and development of human resources from a long-term perspective. Particularly for small and medium-sized water supply operating under strained financial conditions and critical personnel shortages, it becomes necessary to consider the proper scale of future operations and to urgently develop measures for strengthening their management foundation through facility planning, financial planning, and human resource planning.

Management Related to Things

To ensure the provision of water utility services, entailing the stable and affordable supply of safe and palatable water, it is fundamental to appropriately manage the water supply systems and related infrastructures. This is the essence of managing tangible assets.

Herein, we present specific strategies to address these challenges.

1. Enhancing the Emergency Response Capacity against Natural Disasters (Anti-Catastrophe Concept)
The concept of "resilience to crisis" was introduced in the guidelines for earthquake-resistant water facility construction, revised in 2022. In essence, the concept refers to the capability of maintaining uninterrupted services even during unforeseen events. For water utilities, this involves augmenting the emergency response capabilities of individual components such as earthquake-proofing infrastructure and flood mitigation measures (preventive measures to minimize potential damage). Concurrently, in case of damage, measures like system backups and emergency water supply (post-event measures to minimize service disruption when damaged) should be emphasized to prevent a halt in the supply of treated water. As preventive actions, it is crucial to efficiently draft and promote seismic retrofitting plans in tandem with subsequent facility updates. Post-event measures require delineating specific actions during disasters through Business Continuity Planning

(BCP), securing personnel (support-receiving plans), and ensuring resources and equipment (guaranteeing supply chains). Raising awareness through training exercises is also a pivotal part of post-event strategies.

2. Addressing Aging Infrastructure, Obsolescence, and Deterioration
As previously noted, many water facilities developed during the period of rapid economic growth are approaching their renewal phase. The Ministry of Health, Labour and Welfare advocates addressing this issue through asset management, which includes renewal needs, smoothing out renewal demands, and securing renewal funding sources.
Contemplating actual renewal projects involves more than straightforward replacement; upgrades (improving seismic capacity, ensuring backups, etc.) and optimizing scale and capability (downsizing in line with reduced water demand) must be considered, along with reorganization and reconstruction (possible regional consolidation or joint ventures) from a broader perspective.

Management Related to Money

For the sustainable operation of water utilities and the implementation of efficient and effective investments, it is vital to ensure the fiscal health of water utility accounting that underpins the fundamentals of financial management.

Below we describe specific strategies to address the associated challenges.

1. Asset Management and Management Strategy
The Ministry of Health, Labour and Welfare emphasizes the importance of asset management, while the Ministry of Internal Affairs and Communications advocates the formulation of management strategies. These strategies should consider projections affecting public enterprise accounting, such as infrastructure investments (Article 4 budget) and water demand trends (revenues from water supply). Crafting a long-term fiscal balance forecast, understanding the extant problems and tasks, and specifying immediate and short-term actions are indispensable to upholding the integrity of public enterprise accounting. Notably, the formulation of asset management and business strategies is not a one-time event; it is imperative that they be employed in a PDCA (Plan-Do-Check-Act) cycle and be leveraged for deliberating on water utility management policies.

2. Optimization of Water Rates and Pricing Structures
Despite diminishing water demand revenues and rising investments for aging infrastruc-

ture, we see instances where water rates have remained unchanged for prolonged periods, occasionally influenced by election promises and other political considerations. To ensure the health of water utility operations, it is crucial to consider a long-term fiscal outlook and deliberate on optimizing water rates. Furthermore, given the shifts in water demand patterns, there is a pressing need to validate the current pricing structure and reassess if necessary. For instance, many water utilities adopt a progressive water rate system, as a remnant from times when water demand was surging and securing sources was a challenge. Ideally, fixed costs should be steadily recouped through basic charges. Yet, numerous utilities recoup fixed costs via variable charges. A relaxation of the progressive water rate system or the introduction of a degressive water rate system could promote sounder water usage; the proper balancing of basic and volumetric charges is also essential. Transitioning from a water rate system by customer class to a water rate system by mater size would better align with actual water usage patterns.

3. Securing Funding
Rather than solely relying on the current generation's burden based on water rate revenues, it is paramount that various funding sources be utilized, including revenue bonds, grants, and subsidies, to secure the capital necessary for infrastructure development.
However, since corporate bonds entail obligations for future generations, a balanced approach is necessary.

Management Related to People

To provide appropriate services through the operation and management of water supply services and water supply facilities, it is fundamental to build an organization and mechanisms for training and securing talented personnel with the requisite skills. This is the core of human resource management.

Here, we outline specific measures to address these challenges.

1. Recruitment, Development, and Organizational Strengthening
In the water industry, there are few cases of independent recruitment, and job rotation with general departments is employed, making it difficult to continuously secure the quantity and quality of experienced personnel. It is also necessary to adopt methods such as regional collaboration with the government and public-private collaboration. Moreover, the continuous implementation of measures contingent on a basic policy of talent development is vital and requires efforts in talent management, organizational management, and overall

human resource management.

2. Wide Area Management and Wide-Ranging cooperation
Regionalization promotion plans are being formulated by prefectures, and regionalization and regional collaboration are considered as one method of securing and cultivating talented personnel. Even if difficult for an individual water service provider to secure and nurture such talent, optimization of personnel allocation is possible from a broader perspective.

3. Public-Private Partnership
Effective utilization and mutual utilization of the entire water industry's human resources and technical strength are required to improve technological inheritance and operational efficiency.
Partnerships should be promoted, using the skills and know-how available to both water utilities and private operators, aiming for future improvements in technical levels, service levels, and customer satisfaction. Various forms of PPP (Note 4) are available, and PFI can be selected in connection with funding. Cost reduction effects can also be expected.

Conclusion

We have focused on the urgent matters to be addressed in the management of public enterprises (water supply services), but it is necessary to start considering and undertaking the following matters in the near future.

1. Consideration of Local Water Supply Circumstances
The provision of drinking water has always been a basic requirement, and the government has promoted the diffusion and maintenance of water supply facilities through financial support. With the passage of time, however, the cost of upgrading these aging facilities becomes a heavy burden. Alternative water supply methods, such as home delivery and mobile water treatment, must be considered when enormous maintenance and renewal costs grow challenging.

2. Utilization of CPS (Note 5) / IoT (Note 6) (Smart Meters, Etc.)
Challenges including the time-consuming identification of leak locations during disasters, and the extensive time and cost required for maintenance in geographically challenging areas, call for the utilization of cutting-edge technologies like CPS/IoT for automation and early leak detection.

3. Economic Security Legislation (Strengthening the Supply Chain)
The Economic Security Promotion Bill, decided by the Cabinet on February 25,2022, requires attention as the water supply services is included in the core infrastructure.

The basic concepts of managing the resources of people, things, and money are the same for any public enterprise. It is essential to have "money" to maintain "things" that provide services, "people" to utilize them accordingly, and "things" to generate money for continued public enterprises; "people" are also necessary to run a public enterprise properly and "money" crucial to secure and nurture the "people" required to operate public enterprises. This chapter focuses on the water supply services, and while the points set out may not coincide with the actual situations of individual water supply services, if they become the starting point for thinking, inspiring imagination, and contributing to the vision of a wonderful future for the water supply services, it would be our pleasure.

References

※e-GOV Legislation Search, link
※Ministry of Health, Labour and Welfare (MHLW) (2022, March 9), materials from the National water supply services Officers Meeting for Fiscal 2021, link
※Ministry of Health, Labour and Welfare (MHLW) (2022, November 30), Training Materials for water supply services Technical Managers for Fiscal 2022, link
※The Japan Water Works Newspaper (2022, September 5), Water Administration Transfer, Issue No. 5755, p. 1
※Ministry of Health, Labour and Welfare (MHLW) (2022, March 4), Status of Earthquakes
※Resistance in the Water Supply Services for Fiscal 2020, link
※Ministry of Health, Labour and Welfare (MHLW) (2013, March), New Water Vision (Revised Edition 2012), link
※Ministry of Health, Labour and Welfare (MHLW) (2009, July), Guidelines on Asset Management in the Water Supply Services, link
※Ministry of Internal Affairs and Communications (MIC) (2019, March 29), Management Strategy Formulation & Revision Guidelines, link
※Ministry of Internal Affairs and Communications (MIC) (2022, January 25), Management Strategy Formulation & Revision Manual, link
※Japan Water Works Association (2015, February), Guidelines for Calculating Water Charges, link

Notes:

1. DBO (Design Build Operate) refers to the method where the water supply services provider funds the project and undertakes comprehensive tasks such as facility design, construction, and operation management.
2. PFI (Private Finance Initiative) encompasses the comprehensive execution of various tasks such as design, construction, maintenance, and repair of public facilities by leveraging the finances and expertise of private enterprises.
3. BCP (Business Continuity Planning) is the planning process for minimizing damage and ensuring business continuity or recovery during emergencies, such as disasters. The activities of formulating, operating, and continuously improving these plans are referred to as Business Continuity Management (BCM).
4. PPP (Public Private Partnership) represents the concept and approach of collaborating with the private sector to

utilize its diverse expertise and technology. This partnership aims to improve public services, make efficient use of fiscal funds, and streamline operations.

5. CSP (Cyber Physical System) involves collecting data from the physical world using sensor systems, analyzing this data in cyberspace with computer technology, and quantitatively applying the results to various industries, rather than relying on experience or intuition.

6. IoT (Internet of Things) describes a system where not only computers but all products, including smartphones, tablets, and household appliances, become sensor-equipped devices, transmitting vast amounts of data on the internet.

Chapter 12

Actual State of the Designated Administrator System

Shiga University, Koji Yokoyama

Introduction

The Designated Administrator System and the Private Finance Initiative (PFI) are representative methods for introducing private-sector vitality to public facilities as well as collaboration between citizens and government. Both systems were created about 20 years ago, and various problems have emerged today, ranging from the selection of operators to facility management. Many cases have arisen where administrative staff lack the proper understanding of the Designated Administrator System and PFI, leading to problems between the administration and private-sector operators.

In this chapter I will provide an overview of the Designated Administrator System and outline the important points at each phase, from consideration of introduction to handover after project termination while citing actual examples.

Development of the Designated Administrator System

The Designated Administrator System, a scheme established by the Local Autonomy Act amendment in June 2003 (enacted in September), allows any "corporations or other organizations designated by an ordinary local public entity" to manage public facilities, according to Article 244-2, paragraphs 3 to 11, of the Local Autonomy Act. In other words, this system enables public facilities to be managed by any "corporations or other organizations," but it only came into existence after several amendments to the Local Autonomy Act regarding the commissioning of public facility management. This is why even today, cases different from conventional management commissions are incorrectly understood and confusing. Let's first look at the history of these amendments.

The first amendment was passed in 1963. Article 244 of the Local Autonomy Act had long stipulated "public facilities," but paragraph 3 of Article 244-2 was added to state, "When it is recognized as necessary to achieve the purpose of the establishment of public facilities effectively, an ordinary local public entity may entrust the management to a public entity or public-like entity." Here, "public entity" refers to "local public entities, public unions, corporation juridical persons, etc." and "public-like entity" refers to "agricultural cooperatives, chambers of commerce and industry, the Red Cross Society, youth groups, women's associations, school corporations, neighborhood associations, autonomous associations, etc." Today, many local governments introduce management commissions or the Designated Administrator System to such entities, and the origin of public facility management begins here. However, a significant feature of management commissioning is that the consignee is limited to public entities or public-like entities.

A second amendment in 1991 involves paragraph 3 of Article 244-2: "When an ordinary local public entity recognizes the need to achieve the establishment of public facilities efficiently, it may entrust the management to a corporation in which an ordinary local public entity has invested, or a public entity or public-like entity, according to the provisions of the ordinance." Here, "corporation" means "a corporation in which an ordinary local public entity has invested more than half of the capital, basic funds, etc." or "those deemed unproblematic considering the status of investment, dispatch of personnel, etc., and relationships with ordinary local public entities as defined by ministry ordinance." These are the so-called "quasi-governmental organizations" of local public entities. As in the case of public-like entities, there are many examples of quasi-governmental organizations becoming consignees of management commissions or the Designated Administrator System, and it can be said that they originate here. Today, there are cases where local governments non-competitively select designated administrators for the survival of quasi-governmental organizations, an action that impairs healthy competition. These problems are being pointed out and will be discussed later.

At the same time as the expansion of consignees, the introduction of a usage fee system, decision-making on management trustee fees, reporting requests, investigations, and direction rights by local public entities were also established as significant features.

In line with these developments, the Designated Administrator System was finally created in 2003 through an amendment to Article 244-2, paragraphs 3 to 11, of the Local Autonomy Law. Detailed features will be explained later, but it is now possible for any corporations or other organizations to manage public facilities. At the same time, local public entities as investors and shareholders hold supervisory rights over quasi-governmental organizations, and these organizations are subject to audit by an auditor (Article 199, paragraph 7, of the same law); reporting requests, investigations, and direction rights from the local public entity's side are also applicable to designated administrators (Article 244-2, paragraph 10, of the same law). These points cannot be overlooked.

What Is the Designated Administrator System and Its Features?

The Designated Administrator System can be succinctly defined as a system where the "management and operation of public facilities, previously limited to local governments and their affiliated organizations, can now be comprehensively delegated (as an administrative measure and not a commission) to entities including corporations, profit-making companies, foundation corporations, NPO corporations, and citizens' groups." There are three main characteristics within this definition.

The first characteristic is that "management authority related to public facilities is delegated to organizations that receive the designation." Let's look at this in detail. The so-called "designated action" is "an act in which a local government unilaterally appoints a designated administrator as the managing entity of a public facility instead of its creator." This action is treated not as a "contract" but as an "administrative measure." Then, the designated administrator, authorized by the local government, conducts not only factual acts management tasks but also managerial tasks related to residents' rights and obligations. However, these management tasks are limited to "routine administrative measures with minimal authority," such as granting permission for use, revocation, and eviction orders.

The second characteristic is that "the designated administrator can execute permissions corresponding to administrative measures, including usage permits." This is proportional to the first point, but with public facility management, there are "factual acts of management, such as cleaning, maintaining and inspecting facilities," as well as "managerial tasks related to residents' rights and obligations, such as granting permission for facility rental." The former can be privately contracted without being prescribed by ordinance, while the latter requires private contracting based on ordinance.

Thus, a significant feature distinguishing the Designated Administrator System from previous management commissions is that it encompasses not only factual management but also certain authoritative acts (usage permits). However, the power to permit usage includes "granting or denying use, revocation, restriction or cessation, and eviction orders against nuisance users," but it does not allow "forced collection of usage fees, levying of fines, unauthorized usage permits, decisions against objections, or forcible exclusion of wrongful users" by the designated administrator.

The third is "the designated administrator can collect fees from users as revenue within the framework defined by ordinance (i.e., usage fee system)." This system was allowed for management trustees with the 1991 amendment to the Local Autonomy Act and has been inherited by the Designated Administrator System. Designated administrators can set usage fees within the range prescribed by ordinance, with approval from the local government. Fee reduction is also possible, but setting and handling fees is determined by ordinance, and designated administrators can only reduce fees within those limits.

Differences between Task Commissioning, Management Commissioning, and the Designated Administrator System

Let's summarize what differentiates the previous "task commissioning," "management commissioning," and the Designated Administrator System (refer to Table 12-1). First, in terms of the "contracting entity," there are no restrictions in task commissioning, though prohibitions apply to mayors and council members. Management commissioning is limited to "public entities, public organizations, and corporations defined by ordinance (1/2 or

Table 12-1

	Outsourced Operations	Conventional Administrative	Outsourcing Specified
Contracted/Entrusted Entity	No restrictions ※ Prohibition of holding concurrent mayor and council member positions. (Local Autonomy Act, Articles 92-2, 142)	Limited to public bodies, quasi-public bodies, and investment corporations as defined by ordinance (with 50% or more investment).	Corporations and other organizations ※ Corporate status is not necessarily required, but individuals are not permitted. Legal nature
Legal Nature	"Contractual relationship under private law" Entrusting individual administrative tasks or operations based on a contract.	"Contractual relationship under public law" Entrusting specific management tasks or operations based on a contract concluded in accordance with legal nature ordinances.	"Management delegation" "Designation" (a type of administrative disposition) entrusts the authority to manage public facilities to the designated person.
Authority over Public Facilities	Owned by the local public entity that established them.	Owned by the local public entity that established them.	Owned by the designated administrator. ※ Standards of management and scope of operations are defined by ordinances. Specific contents are defined in an "agreement."
Permission for Public Facility Use	Contractor cannot permit.	Contractor cannot permit.	Designated administrator can permit.
Usage Fee System	Contractor cannot permit.	Contractor cannot permit.	Designated administrator can permit.
Damages Compensation	Liability for Damages Responsibility of the city. (State Redress Act, Article 2, paragraph 1)	Responsibility of the city, but if damage is attributable to the management contractor, the city has the right of recourse. (State Redress Act, Article 2, paragraph 2)	Responsibility of the city, but if damage is attributable to the designated administrator, the city has the right of recourse. (State Redress Act, Article 2, paragraph 2)

Source: "On the Introduction and Operation of the Designated Administrator System for Public Facilities" (Based on the author's work in the Minamishimabara City Planning Promotion Department, Planning and Promotion Division, September 2017, (Heisei 29))

more investment, etc.)." The Designated Administrator System includes corporations and other organizations, so legal personality is not always necessary, but individuals are not allowed.

Second is "legal nature." "Outsourced operations" constitute a "contractual relationship under private law." This involves entrusting individual administrative tasks or operations based on a contract. "Conventional administrative outsourcing" is a contractual relationship under public law that involves entrusting specific management tasks or operations based on a contract concluded in accordance with the legal nature ordinances. The Designated Administrator System becomes "management delegation" that involves entrusting the authority to manage public facilities to a designated person through "designation" (a type of administrative disposition).

Regarding "authority over public facilities," in both outsourced operations and conventional administrative outsourcing, the local public entity establishing the facility holds the authority. In the Designated Administrator System, the designated administrator retains the authority. In this context, the "standards of management" and the "scope of operations" are defined by ordinances, and the specific contents are set out in an "agreement."

Third, for "permission for public facility use," neither "outsourced operations" nor "conventional administrative outsourcing" contractors can give permission of use. The Designated Administrator System allows the designated administrator to do so.

Fourth, the "usage fee system" cannot be adopted for outsourced operations, but can be adopted for both conventional administrative outsourcing and the Designated Administrator System.

Lastly, for outsourced operations, "liability for damages" is the responsibility of the local public entity (State Compensation Act, Article 2, paragraph 1). In conventional administrative outsourcing and the Designated Administrator System, liability for damages is, in principle, the responsibility of the local public entity, but for damage attributable to the management contractor or the designated administrator, the local public entity has the right of recourse (State Compensation Act, Article 2, paragraph 2).

Points to Consider in Each Phase

The Designated Administrator System typically follows the process of consideration for introduction → amendment of the establishment management ordinance (resolution) → public recruitment (creation of recruitment guidelines and specifications) → candidate selection (convening a selection committee) → designation of the designated administrator, assuming liabilities (resolution) → conclusion of an agreement with the designated administrator (creation of the agreement documents) → management and operation by the designated administrator → regular monitoring → conclusion of the designated period, and handover.

Almost 20 years have passed since the establishment of this system, and various issues have been raised at each phase. One major factor is the lack of strict legal definition of the Designated Administrator System, with its actual operation largely at the discretion of local governments. Given the cases of its improper use, I would like to discuss the several points related to the operation of the Designated Administrator System based on my personal experience.

① Consideration for Introduction

Initially, there is consideration of whether or not to introduce the Designated Administrator System to a given facility. The main perspectives of this consideration can be summed up in three points. The first is consideration from a policy standpoint. For instance, the local government must consider the role of a tourist facility within its tourism policy. While seemingly obvious, there are cases where the administration fails to consider this point, expecting private businesses to provide insights through their proposals. Private enterprises should build upon the policies set by the local government while offering new ideas; it is a misunderstanding to expect private enterprises to consider what the administration should be doing. The second point involves financial considerations, particularly evaluating the cost-effectiveness of introducing the Designated Administrator System. It is a mistake to aim only for cost reductions. One benefit of the public-private partnership is the expected overall cost reduction, but excessive cost-cutting may lead to poor working conditions for the private enterprise. Both quantitative and qualitative evaluations, like the unquantifiable positive impacts on the community, should be considered. The third point involves the perspective of private enterprises, essentially, whether there is demand from private enterprises to engage in policy areas related to the facility. Even if the administration wants to entrust the facility to the private sector, an unattractive market will not induce private-sector companies to enter.

② Amendment of the Establishment Management Ordinance

Once the decision to introduce the Designated Administrator System is made, the next consideration is whether the establishment management ordinance should be amended, which involves three main considerations. The first consideration is from a public facility management standpoint, that is, can facilities be integrated or combined? The need to reduce public facilities managed by public entities will be essential in light of future financial burdens. It will be necessary to select designated administrators who can address multiple policy areas or consider joint ventures of multiple companies. Second, it is essential to consider the most appropriate form, for example, deciding whether the introduction of the Designated Administrator System is appropriate, or if consignment or direct management would be better. The third point is revisiting the purpose of establishment. The increasing complexity of public facilities today may create the need to revise traditional establishment objectives to fully leverage the skills and expertise of private enterprises. Local governments should be flexible in making timely revisions in line with modern times.

③ Public Recruitment Period

Next, we will examine the recruitment guidelines and specifications. There are three points to consider at this stage. The first is whether the division of roles between the administration and private operators is clearly outlined. Although distinction and risk-sharing between designated management projects and independent projects are proportional, even before that, some municipal administrations act as third-parties when introducing the Designated Administrator System. However, the principal actors of public policy are the municipalities themselves, and ignoring this responsibility is a mistake. There might be concerns about disguised subcontracting, but since the designated administrator operates according to municipal policy, it does not mean that the municipality is responsibility-free. I would like the administration to fulfill its role properly.

The second point, as previously mentioned, is whether the recruitment guidelines and specifications are appealing to private operators. In recent years, the entrenchment of designated administrators has become problematic, one reason for which may be the lack of revision to the recruitment guidelines and specifications since the initial period. Without such change, designated administrators entrenched in their position can easily gain an unfair advantage. Related to this is the third point: whether the recruitment guidelines and specifications enable new entrants. By including new content, current designated administrators will have to step up their efforts, and it can also become an incentive for businesses aiming to enter the field.

④ Selection Process

Once the preparations are complete, the selection committee is convened. There are many issues with the committee members. First, whether the members of the selection committee are appropriate. My experience has seen many cases where specialists are entirely lacking. While including residents who represent users is beneficial, it is important to have legal experts such as lawyers, accountants including CPAs and tax accountants, and experts in local autonomy and the Designated Administrator System. Indeed, I encountered one case where a business operator withdrew before contract deliberation after being selected for preferential negotiation rights without its finances being examined by an expert. This incident occurred because an accounting expert had not been appointed to the committee.

Furthermore, it is crucial to share necessary information with appointed committee members for subsequent evaluations. Otherwise, committee members may ask confusing questions during a business operator's presentation or use different scoring criteria, resulting in biased evaluation scores.

There are also problems with how the selection committees operate, for example, disclosing a business operator's presentation, leaking information to competing businesses in attendance, or a business operator recording the Q&A session with committee members. These are not abstract issues regarding the Designated Administrator Selection Committee but actual occurrences.

Moreover, many problems are observed with the evaluation methods. There is an urgent need to clarify standards, such as the minimum points for meeting requirement levels. In some instances, decisions are based on discussions among committee members, rather than by totaling or averaging the scores. Such practices should be avoided to prevent the suspicion of arbitrary decisions.

⑤ Designation and Agreement Conclusion
At the time of designation and agreement conclusion, I would like to point out three main considerations.

First, the focus should be on the "details of the agreement." An agreement is equivalent to a private contract, making it of paramount importance. Details not specified in ordinances must be stipulated in the agreement. At the heart of this are arrangements concerning designated management tasks, independent projects, and proportionate designated management fees and user fees. However, there are instances where the boundary between a designated management task and an independent project is vague, or where the range of the designated management fee is interpreted differently by the administration and the designated administrator (private operator). A common misconception is to refer to the tasks performed at the discretion of the designated administrator within the designated management tasks as independent projects. For instance, if lifelong learning courses at a community center are designated management tasks, but the contents of the courses are left to the designated administrator's discretion, they remain designated management tasks and not independent projects. Not clearly defining such fundamental terms can lead to future complications, making it is essential to clarify the scope of each project and the associated funding sources.

Furthermore, some municipalities put in place agreements that require designated administrators to remit part of their revenue to the local public entity establishing the facility, essentially returning a portion of the profits. While there are no legal provisions regarding profit-sharing, many instances exist in practice, the extent to which could significantly inhibit the incentives for private operators. At a minimum, the sharing ratio should be set at a level acceptable to the public. One extreme example I encountered was an agreement where the municipality did not pay the designated management fee, covering all expenses from the user fees collected by the designated administrator, and further required an annual fixed payment of 50 million yen, plus an additional 50 percent of the annual profit. What private operator would take on such conditions? This approach suggests that the municipality did not understand the purpose of the Designated Administrator System. The introduction of private-sector vitality is not about using the private sector cheaply, and while there is no need to overemphasize private operators, public facilities must be operated in an equal partnership with the public sector to ensure a wholesome collaboration.

Conversely, if designated management fees generate a surplus due to the negligence of obligatory tasks unrelated to business efforts, the surplus in principle should be returned, or alternatively, the surplus could be diverted to other projects. In any case, it is vital to predetermine the handling of revenue and surplus.

Second is the focus on "risk sharing." There are various risks with financial fluctuations, price fluctuations, economic environment, residents' responses, third-party compensation, facility defects, and defaults. Risk sharing involves predetermining which party, the administration or the designated administrator (private operator), deals primarily with these risks, who bears the responsibility, and who incurs the costs. This allocation is often documented in a risk-sharing table. Historically, many municipalities have lacked awareness regarding risk sharing. Actual risks might not be felt until they manifest. However, the importance of risk sharing became evident during the COVID-19 pandemic. As a force majeure, the pandemic caused a decline in revenues for many facilities and raised compensation issues. Due to a lack of prior experience, many municipalities hurriedly calculated compensation amounts. Recently, the recommendation is not just to have a risk-sharing table, but also to decide on subsequent measures. While few municipalities are fully prepared, it is crucial to plan as best possible. Besides compensation, penalties for cases where the designated administrator withdraws before the specified period must also be established.

Third we address the "consultation clause." Typical agreements often include clauses such as, "Matters not specifically provided for shall be determined upon consultation between the city and the designated administrator." While indispensable, over-reliance on this clause implies that all uncertainties can be addressed later through consultation. Often, these consultations lean more towards requests from the administration to the designated administrator, which can lead to various issues. The above mentioned risk sharing is a prime example. While it is challenging to anticipate all risks, it is essential to discuss foreseeable scenarios, establish basic approaches for handling them, and consistently strive to organize these considerations.

⑥ Management and Operation Period

I would like to highlight the following three points related to management and operation. The first point addresses the "command and control authority." The government cannot directly order the employees of a designated administrator. Only the responsible persons of the designated administrator can issue direct orders to its employees. This problem becomes most apparent during disasters. When a disaster occurs it is necessary to determine the extent to which the designated administrator, as a private business operator, must assume responsibility, and to agree on the division of roles. Designated administrators are also responsible for ensuring the safety of their employees. Generally, the initial disaster rescue and relief efforts are the roles of the designated administrator, while subsequent relief, facility suspension, and restoration are the local government's responsibility.

The second point concerns "maintenance and repair costs." The most common management and operation problems arising between local governments and designated administrators are related to these costs. A typical agreement might state, "The designated administrator shall bear the cost of minor repairs up to approximately 300,000 yen." However, disputes often arise due to unclear interpretations or ambiguous criteria for this threshold. In one example I observed, an attempt was made to classify the multimillion-yen renewal of an elevator as "repair" and make the designated administrator responsible for the cost. This can be seen as a typical example of administrative staff failing to understand what maintenance and repair costs are, and by extension, what the Designated Administrator System is. It is necessary for the local government to organize expectations for the scope and cost burden of maintenance and repairs, similar to risk-sharing. Essentially, facility maintenance is the responsibility of the local government.

The third point concerns "damage compensation." In cases where both the local public body and the designated administrator have breached their obligations, they can claim damages against each other under the provisions of the Civil Code. However, as for liability to users of public facilities, Articles 1 and 2 of the State Redress Act apply. Article 1 states, "When a public official acting on behalf of the state or a public body intentionally or negligently causes harm to another person, the state or public body is responsible for compensation," and Article 2 states, "If a person suffers damage due to defects in the establishment or management of roads, rivers, or other public constructions, the state or public body is responsible for compensation." In such cases, the local public body has a liability to third parties, but if the designated administrator is responsible for unlawful acts, the local public body can seek compensation from the designated administrator.

⑦ Monitoring Period
There are three types of monitoring: ① Voluntary monitoring by the designated administrator, ② Monitoring by the local public body (facility management division), and ③ Monitoring by a third party (external audits, etc.).

Local public bodies must conduct appropriate monitoring based on specifications, agreements, and risk-sharing tables. As I mentioned earlier, specifications, agreements, and risk-sharing tables are essential. It is improper to demand unstipulated items from the designated administrator, while stipulated items not complied with must be corrected. To my knowledge, there are local governments that do not conduct this type of monitoring as well as local governments that only conduct one of the three types of monitoring.

Similarly, many local governments do not prepare monitoring sheets (evaluation sheets) or establish systems like the Designated Administrator Evaluation Committee. Ideally, instead of leaving the task to each department, the department in charge of reform should lead regular monitoring across the entire organization. Beyond internal monitoring by local public bodies, specialists in local autonomy, law, accounting, and other fields should also be included in the Designated Administrator Evaluation Committee and other such bodies, with external evaluations (audits) conducted from a professional standpoint. It is not uncommon for the Designated Administrator Selection Committee to also serve as an evaluation committee.

⑧ End of Term and Handover Process

Finally, I will discuss a number of points related to the "end of term and handover." Since this concerns matters that arise several years down the road, the issues can be difficult to anticipate, but it is essential that the administration and the designated administrator carefully discuss "restoration to the original state" and the subsequent "handover of tasks" at the conclusion of the initial agreement. Otherwise, with the designation of a new private business operator at the end of the term, the previous business operator may regard the new operator as a competitor. I am aware of cases where private operators treat all information as "trade secrets" and withhold necessary information from subsequent operators. Drawing the line here is incredibly challenging, but it is vital to set out what should be publicly disclosed, stipulating the information to be handed over while protecting intellectual property. Properly executing these tasks at the end of the term and handover will enhance the credibility of the local government, promote healthy competition among private business operators, and encourage new entrants.

References

※Atsushi Miyawaki, Hiroshi Iguchi, and Tatsuya Wakao, "Designated Administrator System Problem-Solving Handbook" (Toyo Keizai Shinposha, 2019)
※Koji Mori, "Practical Work of the Designated Administrator System" (Gyosei, 2021)
※Planning and Promotion Division, Minamishimabara City, "Introduction and Operation of the Designated Administrator System for Public Facilities" (September, Heisei 29)

Chapter 13

Actual State of the Private Finance Initiative (PFI)

Shiga University, Koji Yokoyama

Introduction

The Private Finance Initiative (PFI) stands alongside the Designated Administrator System as one of the principal methods of introducing private-sector vitality to public facilities and fostering public-private partnerships. However, even after over 20 years since its establishment, PFI is not as widespread as the Designated Administrator System. In the field of local government, there seems to be a prevailing misconception that PFI is complicated.

In this chapter I would like to succinctly discuss the key points of PFI. Although PFI and Public-Private Partnership (PPP) in Japan might seem immature, they are not inherently complicated.

The accumulation of knowledge and experience at the local government level allows a system to mature. I strongly encourage local governments to approach PFI with a proactive spirit based on the role they play in shaping the system.

Development of PFI

PFI refers to a method wherein, instead of conventional publicly funded and operated public facilities, private enterprises procure the funding, develop the public facilities, and even manage their subsequent operations. This reform method was first established in the United Kingdom in the 1990s.

In Japan, the situation has continued to evolve since the enactment of the Act on Promotion of the Private Finance Initiative (PFI Act) in 1999, followed by several amendments. Specifically, in the first and second amendments in 2001 (Heisei 13) and 2005 (Heisei 17), the law mainly permitted land development as a private revenue business, along with public facilities. The third amendment in 2011 (Heisei 23) introduced the Public Facility Operation Right (the so-called "concession method"), greatly expanding the PFI scheme by allowing private enterprises to provide services directly to general users in public service businesses such as airports and water supply. Subsequent amendments in 2013 (Heisei 25), 2015 (Heisei 27), and 2018 (Heisei 30) mainly promoted this right, with the introduction of the Public Facility Operation Right to the water supply business in the 2018 amendment gaining significant attention. In the most recent amendment in fiscal 2022, the definition of public facilities subject to PFI projects was expanded to include sports facilities and assembly facilities, and other additions were made. It seems that PFI will continue to seek better forms of public-private partnership through repeated revisions. Meanwhile, the Private Finance Initiative Promotion Office of the Cabinet Office (PPP/PFI Promotion Office) is working to popularize PFI by creating various guidelines, manuals, and collections of examples.

However, as I will discuss later, PFI was not widely adopted until around 2015. The national government, as part of then Prime Minister Abe's key policy, "Abenomics," has put more effort into promoting the PFI policy, encouraging the creation of regional platforms for industry, academia, and government related to PFI and such. I also received national accreditation and established the Omi Public-Private Partnership Research Forum in Shiga Prefecture in 2016. Thanks to these efforts, PFI projects are now common and gaining a foothold in municipalities across Shiga Prefecture, although they have yet to penetrate every municipality.

Current State of PFI Implementation

Now let's take a look at the current nationwide adoption of PFI. According to the PPP/PFI Promotion Office of the Cabinet Office, which releases the relevant data on its website, as of March 2022, a total of 875 projects have been implemented, representing a considerable jump from just three cases when the system began in 1999 (Heisei 11). In a single fiscal year, there are 57 projects, with the numbers gradually increasing since 2015. The concession method has also risen to 41 cases. In proportion, the total contract amount has reached 6,970.6 billion yen and is gradually accumulating.

Furthermore, looking at the cumulative number of policy implementations by field, Education and Culture (social education facilities, cultural facilities, etc.) accounts for 32.6 percent, Urban Development (roads, parks, sewerage facilities, port facilities, etc.) for 24.6 percent, Health and Environment (medical facilities, waste treatment facilities, mortuaries, etc.) for 14.6 percent, Office and Lodging (administrative office buildings, government employee lodgings, etc.) for 8.5 percent, Safety (police facilities, fire facilities, correctional facilities, etc.) for 2.9 percent, Life and Welfare (welfare facilities, etc.) for 2.8 percent, Industry (tourism facilities, agricultural promotion facilities, etc.) for 3.0 percent, and Others (complex facilities, etc.) for 8.7 percent. It is apparent that PFI adoption is advancing in Education and Culture, while its introduction in Others (complex facilities, etc.) is also gradually increasing, and it seems likely that PFI's introduction in complex facilities will continue to expand in the future.

Features of PFI

Let's revisit the concept of PFI. As previously introduced on the website of the Private Finance Initiative Promotion Office of the Cabinet Office (PPP/PFI Promotion Office), "PFI is a new method that involves the construction, maintenance, management, and operation of public facilities, utilizing private funds, management skills, and technical capabilities."

Looking further at the details, specifically, how does the PFI method differ from the conventional method (public construction)? In the "PFI Practice Guidebook for Local Government Officials," issued by the private capital utilization project promotion organization (a government-private fund established under the PFI Act, hereinafter the "Guidebook"), the following four differences are explained.

1. Contractual Form – In the conventional method (public construction), public authorities either handle the design, construction, maintenance, and operation themselves or split orders among private businesses to carry out the project. In the PFI method, the public sector focuses on planning, designing, and monitoring, while private businesses handle everything from design to operation.

2. Ordering Method – Orders are divided in the conventional method (public construction) based on specifications, and short-term contracts are drawn up. The PFI method uses bulk ordering, performance-based ordering, and long-term contracting.

3. Risk Sharing – In the conventional method (public construction), the public sector typically bears the risk, while in public-private contracts the risk is shared.

4. Fund Raising – In the conventional method (public construction), the public sector raises funds through general finances, grants, and bonds, while private businesses raise all or part of the project cost.

From these aspects, the particular features of PFI can be viewed as (1) private financing, (2) bulk ordering, (3) performance-based ordering, and (4) long-term contracting.

Effects of PFI Implementation

So, what are the expected benefits of implementing PFI projects? The PPP/PFI Promotion

Office website highlights the following three points.

1. Provision of High-Quality Public Services at Low Cost – PFI projects can utilize private business managerial know-how and technical capabilities. Efficient risk management and cost reduction through an integrated approach to design, construction, maintenance, and operation are expected, leading to cost savings and high-quality public services.

2. Transformation of Administrative Involvement in Public Service Delivery – With private businesses taking over projects previously handled by the government and local public entities, a new public-private partnership based on an appropriate division of roles is expected.

3. Economic Revitalization through Increased Private Business Opportunities – Entrusting private businesses with projects previously managed by the government and local public entities can create new business opportunities. New opportunities also emerge by collaborating with other revenue-generating businesses and adopting financial methods like project finance, along with the creation of new industries and the promotion of economic structural reforms.

Broadly speaking, these benefits represent the advantages of PFI. The incentives for local public entities to adopt the PFI method align with its four distinct characteristics. Specifically,

① Private Financing – In the conventional method (public construction), the public sector must prepare the funds for initial construction and equipment investment all at once, plus repair costs during operation. In the PFI method, private businesses raise funds and permit installment payments, facilitating planned construction, timely repairs, and fiscal stability.

② Bulk Ordering – The conventional method (public construction) divides the tasks of design, construction, maintenance, and operation among different contractors, requiring significant effort. In the PFI method, orders are usually placed with a Special Purpose Company (SPC), reducing the administrative staff's burden.

③ Performance-Based Ordering – The conventional method specifies detailed requirements and implementation methods, while PFI orders are based on performance requirements and lead to public service improvements.

④ Long-Term Contracting – Unlike the Designated Administrator System lasting around five years, the operational period of PFI projects generally exceeds 15 years, which allows for planned project expansion. However, this timeframe does present challenges when it comes to selecting contractors and the possibility of new businesses entering after 15 years.

Advantages and disadvantages are generally two sides of the same coin, but this should not be a reason for looking at PFI negatively. As highlighted at the start of this book, the ultimate objective is to foster a society underpinned by an equitable partnership between the public and private sectors, a vision that PPP/PFI seeks to realize.

Types of Business Methods

PFI (Private Finance Initiative) methods can be classified in several ways. As mentioned in the previously referenced Guidebook, the initial classification hinges on the "method of recuperating business expenses," from which the following three types are derived.

1. Service Purchase Type: This approach recuperates business expenses through payments received from the public sector (ordering party) for delivering public services. Examples include government buildings, school facilities, meal centers, and public housing.

2. Self-Financing Type: This approach recuperates business expenses solely from user fees or revenues generated by associated businesses for delivering public services. Examples include airports, toll roads, water supply, and parking lots.

3. Mixed Type: This type combines both service purchase and self-financing types, recovering business costs from public service payments and user fees. Museums, art galleries, gymnasiums, concert halls, and complex public facilities fall into this category.

The subsequent classifications center on the nature of facility ownership, which can be further divided into six business methods: ① BTO, ② BOT, ③BOO, ④ BT, ⑤ RO, and ⑥ Concession, using the initials of Build (B), Transfer (T), Operate (O), Own (O), and Rehabilitate (R).

① BTO Method: The construction phase is managed privately, but ownership is transferred to the public upon completion, while operations are undertaken by private entities. This method is the most commonly adopted in Japan.

② BOT Method: As with the BTO method, construction is managed privately. However, ownership remains with the private sector until the project's conclusion, and the same entities also oversee operations.

③ BOO Method: The construction phase is managed privately, with ownership being transferred to the public after completion.

④ BT Method: Construction is private, but ownership is transferred to the public upon completion. Afterward, management and operation decisions fall to the public sector, which can choose between direct management or outsourcing. This method is often seen in public housing.

⑤ RO Method: Repairs are conducted by private entities while ownership stays with the public.

⑥ Concession Method: In this final method, ownership stays public, but the right to operate the facilities is granted to private entities fully entrusted with construction, repairs, and management throughout the operational period.

In theory, under the PPP (Public-Private Partnership) framework, the self-financing concession method may appear ideal. However, in practice this method can prove challenging, leading many to opt for the mixed BTO method. As observed earlier, the adoption of concession methods is gradually rising, making it essential to consider this approach when feasible. It is also crucial to adopt a method that suits the local reality without undue pressure.

Points to Consider in Each Phase

As outlined in the Guidebook, the typical process of a PFI project is as follows: idea proposal, solidification of project details, method consideration, examination of the basic scheme, selection of specific projects, recruitment and selection of operators, contract consideration, project commencement, and finally, project termination. Based on my experience I would like to discuss the points requiring consideration in each phase, similarly to the Designated Administrator System mentioned earlier. The problems lying between the public and private sectors are almost the same as those in the Designated Administrator System.

① At the Time of Proposal: Usually, PFI project proposals are made during the formulation of higher-level plans (e.g., comprehensive plans, comprehensive public facility management plans), private proposals, or when considering the renewal of public facilities and infrastructure managed by each department. Unfortunately, I see and hear of cases, both with the Designated Administrator System and PFI projects, where the details are left to each department, without a view of the overall municipality. Such municipalities often propose higher-level plans lacking in consistency, causing PFI projects to become isolated. A coordinating department is needed to oversee the entire municipality, and to offer advice and support to the original department to ensure the smooth progress of a PFI project.

In such cases, the guidelines that prioritize PFI project considerations across the entire municipality are called "priority consideration regulations." The national government (Cabinet Office) expanded the local public entities required to establish priority consideration regulations from municipalities with populations of 200,000 or more to those with populations of 100,000 or more in June of Reiwa 3, as part of the Guidelines for Prioritizing the Introduction of Various PPP/PFI Methods (Reiwa 3, revised edition). They also requested that even municipalities with populations less than 100,000 take similar measures as needed. Essentially, regardless of population size, the possibility of introducing PFI projects must always be considered when renewing public facilities and infrastructure. Some municipalities have also established guidelines for public-private partnerships, including both hardware and software aspects. All municipalities are encouraged to actively engage in PPP and PFI.

② Specificity of Business Content and Consideration during Method Planning: When proposing a PFI project, the next step to consider is the "specificity of business content and examination of business methods." Specifically, this stage involves the formulation of basic concepts and plans, selection and delegation of public advisors, implementation of feasibility studies, and decisions on business methods. I will also point out the considerations regarding these matters.

First, let's talk about the formulation of the basic concept and basic plan. Unfortunately, there are examples where the basic concept and the basic plan are proportional, but without considering the PFI project when drawing up the basic concept, municipalities come face-to-face with reality when formulating the basic plan, being forced to hurriedly consider the PFI project and start over from the basic concept. This often occurs because the basic concept is either too abstract and unrealistic, neglecting the actual budget and related business strategies, or because PFI experts able to provide valuable insights are not included in the committee. Regardless of whether PFI project methods are ultimately adopted, it is crucial at this stage to consider the implications of executing the project through PFI.

Next, the selection and commissioning of public advisors in PFI projects is critical. The selection should not be based merely on a company's size or its past accomplishments, but rather on its capability to provide accurate advice and detailed project support. The track record of public advisors who conduct feasibility studies is therefore crucial to their selection. In other words, you can trust public advisors who perform accurate feasibility studies. Caution should be exercised with consultants whose Value for Money (VFM) calculations seem overly optimistic or excessively stringent. Finally, among the various PFI business methods, such as BTO and BO, the optimal method for the facility in question is determined.

③ During Basic Scheme Consideration: The following steps involve creating implementation policies, drafting requirement levels, setting up proportional monitoring (evaluation) for basic plan drafts, and drafting business contracts. As mentioned in the previous chapter on the Designated Administrator System, implementation policies and requirement levels in PFI businesses are key to making a facility appealing and encouraging many businesses to participate. Particularly, given that the operation period of PFI projects exceeds the designated period in the management system, the contents of the implementation policies and the requirement levels become especially vital. Similarly, the initial criteria will be the basis for review evaluations, subsequent monitoring evaluations, and leading to business contracts, thus making clear the importance of the initial setting. Conversely, items or levels not set initially must not appear in later evaluations or business contracts.

④ Selection of Specific Businesses, Recruitment and Selection of Operators: Next, specific businesses are selected and the recruitment and selection of operators undertaken. "Selection of specific business" refers to the final decision made by the public facility manager under the PFI law, affirming the introduction of PFI methods as the optimal approach for the target business. The municipality has a responsibility to explain to the council and residents the appropriateness of introducing PFI methods to the facility based on the results of the feasibility study. The process of recruiting and selecting operators is fundamentally similar to the Designated Administrator System. However, the design and construction of a PFI project are targeted, so experts in these fields must be selected as committee members. Attention should be paid to avoid conflicts of interest between the expected applicant operators and the committee members. A thorough examination of the candidates' backgrounds and achievements is necessary to confirm this.

⑤ Conclusion of Business Contracts, Start and End of Business: It is crucial to conclude the basic agreement lying at the heart of the business contract, with full discussions held between the administration and the business operator. Particularly when it comes to risk-sharing, more detailed discussions are warranted due to the extended operating periods and risks related to facility design and construction, factors not present in the Designated Administrator System. Possible risks such as business operators becoming financially distressed and withdrawing should also be anticipated as much as possible. This relates to subsequent monitoring.

Monitoring PFI projects occurs at the facility development, maintenance, and operation stages. Self-monitoring by the SPC, monitoring by the municipality, and external monitoring are considered, along with monitoring by financial institutions lending to the SPC. In recent years, direct agreements between local governments and financial institutions are becoming more common from the perspectives of risk-sharing and monitoring, and proactive use of these agreements is desirable.

At the conclusion of operations, clarifying the termination requirements, conducting final contract inspections, and outlining the procedures for business and facility transfers are crucial. Particularly with unforeseen circumstances like the recent COVID-19 crisis, which could occur before the operating period ends, it is necessary to have clear guidelines on penalties and compensation if the business's continuation is jeopardized by force majeure.

References

※Cabinet Office Private Finance Initiative Promotion Division website, accessed in October 2022: https://www8.cao.go.jp/pfi/
※Private Finance Initiative Promotion Agency, "PFI Practical Guidebook for Local Government Officials" (Chuo Keizai Sha, 2019)
※Takahashi Reiji, "20 Years of PPP/PFI: Current Status and Challenges from the Perspective of Legal and Contractual Affairs" (Nikkei Research Monthly Report, February 2020)
※Cabinet Office Private Finance Initiative Promotion Division, "Guidelines for Prioritizing the Implementation of PPP/PFI Methods" (September, Reiwa 4)
※Private Finance Initiative Promotion Council, "PPP/PFI Promotion Action Plan (revised version, Reiwa 4)" (June, Reiwa 4)

Chapter 14

Utilization of Outsourcing

CareerLink Corporation – Taketo Shima

Introduction

With the advancement of digital technology, changes are emerging in the way local governments conduct their work, such as the formulation of digital government execution plans. In fact, momentum is growing in the field to promote the use of RPA, AI and other technologies to advance efficiency. On the other hand, there is an increasing amount of work that local governments must urgently carry out, such as measures against infectious diseases and support for the impoverished.

To achieve local government BPR while responding to unplanned, unpredictable changes, it is important to focus on core operations. Private companies must formulate strategic resource allocation (i.e., strategy) with a clear focus on coping with numerous issues and changes in a competitive environment with limited resources (people, goods, and money). Outsourcing has a history of being used to achieve this. Furthermore, with the mandatory disclosure of human capital starting in fiscal 2023, changes are expected to be seen in the relationship between organizations and the people working in them. These changes will likely have a significant impact on an organization's ability to attract talent (the ability to acquire or retain talented personnel within the organization), and consequently on organizational competitiveness and sustainability. This is becoming the current consensus. Including outsourcing, the diversification of external utilization is an option with certain policies becoming indispensable for the realization of organizational strategies.

However, local government utilization of outsourcing tends to focus solely on "cost reduction per unit task," and commissioning itself is sometimes seen as the goal. Instead, it should be implemented within the local government organization as part of the mechanism to promote organizational development and sustainability, which is the original purpose. In other words, strategic BPR (Business Process Reengineering, or fundamental improvement and reform) aimed at enhancing competitiveness, as in private companies, should ideally include options for external utilization such as outsourcing, and be actively pursued.

In this chapter I will first describe the approach to preliminary preparations for local governments to utilize outsourcing, examine recent changes in the environment surrounding organizations, and discuss changes in the context of expected results from external resources. Next, we will apply the "smile curve" concept used in manufacturing to white-collar work, and show how to consider the essential question of "What is the core business?"

when using external resources. And finally, we will discuss the issues related to "business organization" that tends to stumble when utilizing outsourcing, hopefully in the context of achieving local government BPR.

Changes in the Environment Surrounding Organizations

The BPO market continues to grow steadily in both IT and non-IT businesses. Previously, changes in cost per unit task were the main focus of external utilization, but recently, with changes in the competitive environment and increasing diversification, there has been a rise in outsourcing that focuses more company employees on core tasks. This appears to be supported by the long-term difficulty in securing human and other resources, and in expanding systems and environments that promote the division of labour, such as cloud systems and remote work environments.

Moreover, the disclosure obligation concerning "human capital" will begin in fiscal 2023, initially with listed companies. Disclosure based on the Corporate Governance Code, which mandates consistent disclosure to the market either by "complying or explaining," will naturally lead to changes in the actual operation of various HR systems. Specifically, the introduction of the so-called JOB-type personnel system is partially underway, promoting efforts in various areas such as reskilling, diversity assurance, successor development systems, and sustainability-related items. The era of "get a position or high salary as the years go by" in membership-type employment is coming to an end, urging systematic changes to pay more generous compensation to workers able to produce specialized outputs at higher levels. Also, employees in the so-called "general jobs" will be expected to take on the position of professionals within an organization, and outcomes such as reduction and quality improvement in decision-making and internal coordination costs can be expected. To cope with rapid changes in the competitive environment, responsibilities, roles, and authority will likely be distributed more than ever to teams led by or composed of specialized personnel.

Management and senior executives are now increasingly faced with the need to engage in strategic tasks, for instance, ensuring more advanced governance, maintaining competitiveness, aligning social significance with strategy, considering sustainability, and accelerating decision-making. Consequently, some of the decision-making and core judgments they previously handled will likely be carried out by various teams within the organization and closer to the front lines. As the scope of responsibility and authority expands within teams and projects, the need arises to handle exceptions that used to be delegated upward within the team itself. Hence, there is a motivation to outsource resources related to routine tasks and associated management efforts, leading to "we want to systematize it, we want to outsource it," sentiments that become a trigger for increased external utilization like outsourcing.

In this way, as the roles and expectations that organizations demand from their personnel change, the market value of talented workers with high potential who can deliver more advanced and specialized results increases, and job mobility accelerates, making it no stretch to imagine the fierce competition to acquire the most talented human resources. Factors beyond compensation, such as "scale and discretion of work," "difficulty and rarity," "social value," "workplace environment and work style," and "career development potential," become incredibly important incentives that organizations can (and must continue to) present to workers. Major corporations are advancing initiatives related to human capital management, and organizations must respond to the changing expectations of talented employees.

With organizations throughout the world moving in this direction, failure to adapt, including by local government bodies, may lead to the inability to attract talent. Environments different from the past, such as cloud computing, horizontal division of labour, remote work, job-based work, and side jobs, will demand a loosely coupled way of working where separation and integration are possible. Organizations must create environments that concentrate on core tasks and, whether outsourced or not, these tasks must be reorganized with a view to clarifying responsibilities by position, visualizing tasks, and dividing and sharing work accordingly.

Positioning of Outsourcing

Outsourcing has evolved in response to the need to allocate limited resources more effectively and to maintain the development and sustainability of an organization. When considering the use of outsourcing, one might hear the call to "focus on the core business" from contractors during presentations and explanations, as often as advice and guidelines. The notion of what constitutes a "core business" is incredibly important when utilizing outsourcing. Without a firm understanding of this concept, the process may be reduced merely to a means of staff reduction or superficial cost-cutting, without focusing on the benefits that should ideally be obtained.

First, outsourcing is the act of specifying, contracting, and paying an external vendor to perform tasks that the company has been doing or must do. Since the company pays an external vendor to perform tasks that could otherwise be handled in-house, there must be tangible benefits to this practice. Generally, outsourcing includes assigning routine, non-differentiated tasks to external vendors experienced in market competition, possibly even transferring assets, not just to reduce costs but also to convert costs from fixed to variable, strengthen resource allocation to the core business, ensure variability in costs, and utilize the external vendor's expertise and technology for operational improvement. The benefits of gaining new insights through collaboration also exist.

In the first place, organizations do not hire and train employees to perform low-value-added tasks that anyone can do, even though there are often a vast array and number of miscellaneous tasks that "someone must do" within an organization. The outstanding management layer of employees should shift the resources allocated to these tasks towards business promotion and planning. Such a shift is becoming increasingly emphasized in today's changing work environment, and from the personnel side, the demand to work in a business providing core value to gain experience and performance is growing. If cost reduction was the sole motive for outsourcing, it would likely only suit large enterprises that can leverage scale advantages; but in reality, it has also become an essential means for small and midsized enterprises to ensure their competitiveness.

Next, strategy and policy are necessary when considering outsourcing. Outsourcing itself is not the end goal; it is a tool on par with external utilization, such as systematization, mechanization, staffing, and consulting services, and a means to achieve business growth and Business Process Reengineering (BPR). BPR is a relatively top-down approach where, after organizing the elements and functions to achieve the strategy, priority and resource allocation policies are determined and processes set up around the goals to be achieved. Within this undertaking, one must discern whether it is better to mechanize (automate) the task for improvement, handle the improvement internally, or change the responsible party externally to ensure variability and reduce management efforts as a more beneficial choice for competitiveness.

When considering these aspects, in the context of achieving local government BPR, it is crucial in the deliberation to utilize outsourcing to return to the original purpose of the BPR policy, define what a "core business" is, consider not only the merits but also the potential demerits and risks that can arise, and outline the subsequent resource allocation policy and outsourcing management system. Moreover, since the tasks are carved out to external vendors and systems beyond the framework of the organization, it is increasingly important to continue assessing the organization's internal tasks.

Focus on Added Value of Tasks

When considering the allocation of resources and rebalancing, what characterizes your organization and what constitutes the core business become the topics of high-level discussions. In the context of administration, such as local governments, I surmise that there is a tendency to become overly comprehensive and to struggle with clearly defining priority goals. First, I recommend organizing at the level of tasks in the field.

The smile curve is a framework used in manufacturing, where the horizontal axis is divided into a series of process classifications, such as "planning and marketing," "design," "manufacturing and operation," "sales," and "maintenance," while the vertical axis plots "added value." The curve depicts a situation where added value is depressed in the intermediate process, and the manufacturing and operation part forms a dipped smile-like shape (refer to Figure 14-1). This implies that the "intermediate part of the process is hard to profit from, even if you work hard, so let's design the business horizontally like outsourcing," or "When competing in that field you must produce scale benefits or you will slowly decline."

If we apply this to an organization and consider the so-called manufacturing and operation part as routine work, or relatively standardized work, we can observe and analyze from the perspective of whether dedicating the organization's resources to these tasks can create fi-

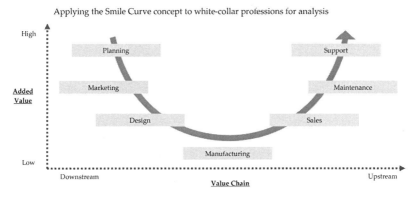

Figure 14-1 (Created by the author)

nancial and non-financial differentiated elements. This analysis helps to organize which processes and tasks add higher value and whether appropriate resources are invested there, not just in terms of superiority or inferiority between business departments (e.g., service execution departments), administrative departments, and planning and support departments, but also within the business departments themselves.

For example, although the difficulty is high, work that is ultimately part of the daily operational tasks is invariably in the category of "manufacturing and operation," while work that involves finding and continually listing, documenting, and maintaining job content, even if the difficulty is low, becomes "maintenance." While the added value and difficulty of each work unit are overwhelmingly higher in the former, envisioning cases where accumulated and organized know-how becomes an inventory list, and the latter leads to significant achievements, may make it easier to organize.

Currently, even in municipalities where outsourcing has been utilized, we see many instances of shortages in the maintenance part of roles. Generally, the number of employees engaged in a project decreases after contracting, but some employees remain to handle project management and tasks requiring authority, as well as high-difficulty cases, as is the norm. Project management staff manage numerical targets and KPI clearances, and discuss recovery measures with contractors in unforeseen circumstances or explore new added value. This process can be viewed as the implementation of planning and design aspects in the field, as in the smile curve concept.

However, concerns such as "throwing and ending" and "vendor lock-in" are often heard, and measures are taken to include "handover clauses" in contracts and specifications, but fundamentally, improving the state where there is a lack of resources in the maintenance part has become a necessary action. Constant monitoring and ensuring that external contractors are doing what is right according to the standards, laws, and regulations, assessing the value provided by the organization, considering what needs to be newly examined, and whether the standards themselves are appropriate are all important tasks even after outsourcing. Nowadays, both the public and the media have grown sensitive. As a result of continuously leaving everything to external contractors, the situation has gone beyond the level of "concern" to the point of significant accidents, and there is a strong sense that maintenance must be strengthened. By utilizing the concept of the smile curve, it becomes easier to organize "what are high-value-added tasks."

In utilizing outsourcing there are many cases where in-house personnel are retained to handle operations for high-difficulty cases, but it is a selectable option to add roles to strengthen the maintenance part, such as "standards personnel" or "maintenance personnel," and assign tasks to promote knowledge sharing with external contractors. Also, when planning the required number of people or costs after the introduction of outsourcing, setting in advance the number of people and costs necessary for roles that "do not yet exist" becomes a fundamental response. In the preliminary examination stage, it is important to understand the added value of the business and to consider what kind of work it is to promote BPR.

What to Outsource

Let's consider the range that can be examined for outsourcing. Generally, the range that can be requested for outsourcing is very wide, and anything can now be outsourced. However, in terms of corporate management, when considering the range of outsourcing with the purpose of "concentrating on the core business and enhancing organizational competitiveness," Peter Drucker has said, "Outsource everything except (top) management" and "Do your strengths in-house, outsource your weaknesses." It is a way of thinking that emphasizes the organization's core business, enhancing the social value provided, and stimulating demand. It is not about outsourcing everything, but recognizing the trap of relying entirely upon it, and Drucker also emphasizes the importance of being prepared to pull back when necessary. In other words, the importance of "maintenance."

Next is the question of "what are the strengths of the company?" This can be represented by focusing on its capabilities (functions and abilities that cannot be performed elsewhere) and the amount of resources invested in tasks located at the top of the smile curve. It can be said that the strategy is to discover the organization's unique functions and abilities, and to consider how to utilize and promote their enhancement. In municipalities, for example, tasks such as formulating policies and plans, and monitoring their progress (similar to project management or steering committees), or promoting collaboration among regional communities or public servants, should be impossible for the private sector to perform. Moreover, as mentioned earlier, maintaining and evaluating outsourced or systematized tasks in legal terms and in light of the organization's priority mission, naturally require judgement of the core tasks. These tasks were not originally eligible for outsourcing and, furthermore, should be considered as strengths, with resource allocation made stronger. It is not just about reducing personnel or costs, but reallocating resources to maintain and promote the sustainability and development of the organization, changing the bearer, and making the organization variable so that it can move flexibly.

In general, potential business activities for outsourcing can be classified along two axes: the vertical axis representing whether the business is "core or peripheral," and the horizontal axis representing whether it is "standard or non-standard." An activity positioned to the right on these axes becomes a candidate for systemization or automation. Items roughly situated in the middle or leaning toward the bottom-right, in the "peripheral and standard" category, are candidates for subcontracting (refer to Figure 14-2). Naturally, the top-left quadrant, or "core and non-standard," corresponds to in-house operations. It is expected going forward that there will be more diversity among the members handling core and non-standard tasks. Moreover, the results sought will likely require more advanced judgments and specialized expertise reflected in the output at the work site. As previously mentioned, some decisions that were once made by management or senior administrators must be executed on-site, or in an environment that can do so, lest rapid changes in the environment or impacts on attracting talented personnel occur. It might be helpful to envision the entire chart shifting towards the top-left. Then, the gaps left by that shift will likely be filled through automation or the utilization of external resources.

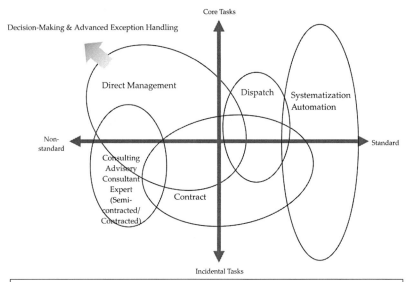

The so-called "core tasks" plotted in the top left are expected to shift further towards decision-making and more advanced exception handling in the future. The idea is to express the entire set shifting further to the top left. Systems are expected to fill this gap, and it is believed that external utilization will come into play.

Figure 14-2. Organization of Task Characteristics by Resource (Created by the author)

Another aspect to consider is the possibility that the primary need for external utilization might be to acquire the appropriate labour. In such cases, the use of specialized external services that provide human resources, such as temporary staffing, could be an option. Although their use is common in the private market, some local governments seem to have no experience in utilizing these services. If only labour is required, it might be more efficient to control it internally as outsourcing even small tasks may lead to excessive management and setup costs. Therefore, a flexible solution to address these challenges might be worth considering. There might also be demands within the organization to resolve its core business activities entirely through external means. In such cases, however, external utilization must be approached carefully by having experts provide the framework, general theories, case studies, or facilitate discussions while internally developing the actual content. Or, internal resources must invest sufficient time in the input and ensure that the output is expertly guided. Without adopting a "let the cobbler stick to his last" mentality, it would likely be challenging to obtain satisfactory results in terms of cost.

Challenges of "Business Streamlining" for Outsourcing

The barriers to the introduction of outsourcing at the municipal level have been clarified by various surveys, with the main items being ① difficulty in streamlining operations, ② difficulty in releasing personal information, ③ difficulty in managing the boundary with disguised subcontracting, ④ concerns about the continuous accumulation of staff know-how, and ⑤ the likelihood of not achieving cost-savings effects. Many cases are halted by internal issues, which is a wasteful situation. I also believe there are structural problems where after the policies of outsourcing and external utilization are determined, planning and design are "thrown" at the field departments. This represents the reality that whether or not outsourcing can be achieved depends on the know-how, arrangement, and winning strategy of the organization, and whether there is enough energy to execute the strategy in the field departments.

These are not peculiar only to local governments, but are also common in general organizations and businesses. However, they tend to become more prominent in a vertically segmented administration. In recent times, considering the Local Government System Standardization Basic Policy, which sets forth business transformation and standardization of systems, utilization of government cloud, and the "service design" concept where the entire service is designed from a customer's perspective, as indicated in the Digital Government Promotion Policy, the probability of business achievement by simply "throwing" the planning and detailed design at a department is quite low. In the private sector, there is a growing shortage of talented personnel who can perform these tasks, and the importance of maintaining resources internally is now recognized. There are many external services that perform PMO (Project Management Office) tasks and business design support, but completely entrusting these tasks to external services may disrupt the continuous inventory and review of operations (i.e.., maintenance), so care must be taken not to overly rely on external services.

In response, given the significant changes in the current situation, there seems to be an active movement to utilize talented personnel who know the tricks of the trade as shared assets within the organization. Even in local governments, I believe it is effective to foster talent with experience in project management and decomposition, visualization, and reconstruction of operations as "BPR coordinators," and to actively involve them in the departments targeted for outsourcing and BPR promotion. This approach can serve as a solution to various challenges that include wholesale delegation, black box implementation, or abandoning externalization / automation altogether.

Many local governments have recently formulated Policies for the Utilization of Private Commissioning, and I think the environment for project promoters in local governments to proceed easily has been created with the establishment of conference bodies for KPI management, efficiency improvements, and specifications of monitoring items. However, these "utilization policies" tend to stall at the "concept-making" stage, focusing on cost reduction and the simultaneous improvement of residents' services, relying on cheaper and higher quality providers to appear in the region. Local governments are often not yet able to look at overall service or business restructuring, but it seems wasteful for these conditions to differ depending on the size and location of the local government.

Nevertheless, as I am stating here, what organizations should focus on when utilizing external resources is, for example, the rebalancing policy of self-owned resources, strengths, organizational mission, reskilling policy for constituent talents, strengthening points for medium-term priority measures, and hidden costs, and addressing these so that the organization can concentrate on its core operations to promote problem-solving. However, these items are rarely found in "utilization policies." It is necessary to consider how the changes in the environment to which organizations are exposed today affect the sustainability of the organization itself, and how these changes should be structured, when possible, with an emphasis on governance.

Inventory of Operations

In the previous chapters we discussed "consideration (concept making)," and it is important to confirm the current situation and design in greater detail after going through this phase. The keys in this process are the inventory of business operations and the list of operations. Entering the design stage in an incomplete state can lead to failures, delays, and additional costs due to missing or leaked business requirements, including contracting requirements. Conversely, if an inventory table and collection of forms are prepared at this stage, it is safe to say that the essential outsourcing requirements will have been met.

When taking an inventory of business operations, the documents typically created include ① business flow of Level 1 to Level 2 (detailed up to Level 3 in some cases), ② collection of forms (input & output collection), ③ system concept diagram & system flow, and ④ list of operations (+ FAQs). As mentioned earlier, these aspects should not be entirely outsourced. However, many sites get hung up at this point, so initially receiving proper support services to advance the organization, aiming to make your own revisions, is a realistic option. This holds true even after outsourcing, and without the organization's involvement at this stage, there may be a black box within the contractor, hindrances to proper management, disadvantages when rolling back operations, and many other disadvantages.

I believe the inventory of business operations eventually converges into a final list of operations. Thus, the way to create the list of operations (how to structure it) is crucial, and attention must be paid to ensure that the basic "MECE" (an acronym for "Mutually Exclusive and Collectively Exhaustive," is a principle used in problem-solving and data analysis) is established. For example, the size of items, large, medium, and small, is aligned by "matching the granularity or level". Even creating rules such as structuring tasks into categories like large system, medium system small system and always compiling exceptions in FAQs can change the efficiency and completeness of the organization.

Once sorted out with the estimated quantity and hours recorded, the organization can be reused directly. By providing a column to specify whether the work will be performed by the contractor or staff, the range to be contracted can be clarified, and consultation and adjustment with the contractor should proceed smoothly. Then, after checking the flow of documents and data, and system permissions, the actual scope of the contract can be finalized, and each structure and communication coordination system determined in order to clear away any legal compliance issues, such as disguised subcontracting. Our company's smooth start-up was realized by disclosing an inventory table and list of operations used as specifications at the start of the contract in a municipality we previously served. We continue to review the list of operations even after outsourcing begins, and I feel the previously mentioned maintenance process is functioning properly.

One point to note in the inventory process is the mistake of overestimating or underestimating the working hours of the candidate tasks to be contracted by simply recording the hearings from the previous task principals. This is not limited to municipalities and happens in various organizations; it is human nature for everyone to think their work is "running efficiently and properly, and that these are important tasks." Therefore, when considering outsourcing, it is advisable to have a third party confirm that the working hours are not overestimated or underestimated to avoid the confusion of rework or lack of working hours after the project begins. It is also important to reconfirm that no mistakes have been made with the executing body or by having a candidate task contracted when it could have been carried out far more efficiently by the staff itself. In any case, overlooking, misjudging quantities or hours, or failing to understand at this stage may boomerang as risks or additional costs once the operation starts. I think it is essential to visualize the work for the future organization's "detachable state" and "loose-coupled organization or way of working." Therefore, I recommend starting an "inventory of business operations," the first and foremost part of business improvement, as soon as possible if it can be done.

Conclusion

When considering outsourcing, merely having the existing operations traced by the contractor is not sufficient to achieve the desired outcome. Moreover, the benefits of outsourcing cannot be enjoyed by imagining "cost reduction using wage disparities," where non-regular private-sector employees are performing staff tasks using the same procedures and management methods. By narrowing down the tasks essential for the staff to carry out, and considering mechanization and the use of external vendors, a continuous improvement management system can be implemented, and the optimization of operations and resource allocation can be achieved.

With the recent advancements of technology, improvement examples in office work by IT investment from contractors during the entrustment period are being seen, and the improvement measures that contractors like our company can implement are diversifying, and the options for proposals are increasing. However, controlling and scrutinizing whether they are the optimal methods or not is an important job for the municipality. Also, based on the assumption that many changes will occur in the future, strengthening resources towards higher value-added work will lead to more efficient administration and greater resident satisfaction in building a system to promote significant administrative services.

Chapter 15

Regional Reform and Intermediate Support

(Community Support & Collaborative Assistance)

Shiga University, Koji Yokoyama

Why Is Regional Reform Necessary?

As stated in Chapter 2, administrative management reform is not confined solely to governmental offices. Only when regional reforms are carried out in conjunction can it be considered complete. So, why is regional reform necessary? I believe there are four major reasons.

First, "inappropriate revenue and expenditure lead to municipal management losses." As we have seen in previous chapters, much of the expenditure, consisting mainly of subsidies, goes to regional residents and organizations. The same applies for revenue. Concessions for public facility usage fees target regional residents and organizations. If subsidies and other financial aid are being distributed in scandalous, inefficient and ineffective ways, it can lead to a loss in municipal management. In other words, taxes are being spent wastefully. If a subsidy, it is necessary to check whether the organization receiving the subsidy is using it properly. If the organization's governance is inappropriate, only rectifying the situation can be considered reform. Subsidies do not end with their distribution.

Second, "under the name of decentralization within cities, regions are exhausted." As also mentioned in Chapter 1, regions are facing a population decline and aging society, leaving them worn out. The most significant issue is the ongoing existence of organizations and systems created during the high economic growth period (population increase phase), despite the lack of human and financial resources. There are cases today where the burden on regions has risen under urban decentralization. We hear complaints from community leaders that requests from the administration keep increasing. In particular, many municipalities are "dumping" excessive tasks onto regional self-governing bodies, such as community councils, even using the Designated Administrator System to manage community centers and other public facilities. This can be called misguided reform and an incorrect introduction of private-sector vitality. Can regional autonomous organizations bear managing and operating public facilities in an era when even maintaining community associations is becoming difficult? Municipalities need to consider more realistic ways of utilizing regional autonomous organizations. Furthermore, municipalities willing to pass off their responsibilities are not promoting true regional self-government and citizen self-government, and are not nurturing regional talent. In other words, there is a lack of intermediate support. Reform is needed here as well. I will discuss this prescription in more detail later.

Third, "system fatigue in existing organizations" can be cited. As mentioned in Chapter 1, scandals involving existing organizations are occurring nationwide. When looking at online news, almost daily we read of embezzlements, falsified reports, thefts by administrative staff in charge of groups, ostracizing of new community members, compulsory membership in fire brigades, compulsory shortfalls, forced withdrawals by welfare commissioners for so-called inspections and trips, and more. Even if actions do not reach the level of scandals, issues such as the excessive burden passed on from the administration to community associations, backdoor budgeting by schools relying on donations from PTAs, vested interests in subsidies to social education organizations, and excessive concession measures are becoming problematic in many municipalities and regions. The essence of these problems lies in the fact that organizations created after World War II cannot meet today's modern challenges and are becoming dysfunctional. It may be time to seriously consider integrating, reorganizing, or rebuilding existing organizations and businesses to meet current needs, and to decide exactly on what our limited human and financial resources should be allocated to.

Fourth, "the lack of proper guidance, advice, and intermediate support from the administration" can be cited. As mentioned earlier, there is a lack of intermediate support, but many administrative staff are obsessed with the idea that they should not intervene in regional autonomous organizations and social education organizations. However, it does not mean that these organizations are extraterritorial.

Despite the intermediate support being provided, we continue to see problematic examples such as playing free with subsidies, supporting only NPOs and not geographically-based organizations, and conducting workshops without resulting improvements. There are also misunderstandings about intermediate support organizations. It is desirable to establish these organizations in each municipality, but it does not mean building grand structures like citizen activity centers. The important point is their function.

Furthermore, there are many tasks the administration should be doing even before setting up an intermediate support organization. As mentioned earlier, checking the destination of subsidies, conducting audits periodically, and proposing reorganization plans for community associations can be performed without intermediate support organizations.

The above points are the main reasons why regional reform is necessary. If regional governance is not appropriate, the implementation of efficient and effective measures becomes an impossible task, and at worst, democracy may suffer. To prevent this situation, it is necessary to carry out reforms, including regional reform, as part of administrative management reform.

The History of Community Policies in Japan

Now, I would like to discuss regional community reform, focusing specifically on community development councils, neighborhood associations (self-governing associations), and other local autonomous organizations. Before we go further, let me briefly touch upon the history of our nation's community policies. The emergence of neighborhood associations dates back to 1889, when the Meiji government implemented the Municipalities Act. With the establishment of modern cities and towns, previous local units were labeled "natural villages," and considered the predecessors to neighborhood associations. However, in the early Showa era, these units were incorporated into the wartime totalitarian system, and in 1940, neighborhood associations were unified as "village associations and neighborhood associations" from the standpoint of "universal support." Furthermore, in 1943, neighborhood associations were legally positioned through the revision of the Municipalities Act. This legal positioning was by no means positive, and it became a significant reason why postwar community policies, including neighborhood associations, have not been legalized to this day. With the end of the war, the occupation forces banned the neighborhood associations in 1947, fearful of the significant role they had played under the totalitarian regime, and this policy continued until 1952.

However, pure regional autonomous organizations like neighborhood associations were probably needed. Later, in line with the high economic growth period, neighborhood associations were revived and evolved while performing quasi-administrative roles, such as distributing newsletters. However, as the 1970s began with high economic growth and increasing urbanization, shadows began to appear in traditional community collaborations. The Ministry of Home Affairs, concerned about this trend, announced the Guidelines for Measures Concerning Communities (Neighboring Societies) in 1971, and designated 83 areas as model community districts. New community measures were initiated, but the efforts did not lead to fundamental community reforms. In the 1980s and 1990s, the Ministry of Home Affairs similarly attempted community measures to replace traditional local autonomous organizations on three occasions, but none saw significant success.

Eventually, as the 2000s arrived, municipal mergers took place along with the decentralization trend. The "Regional Autonomy District & Regional Council System" was established in 2004 through the revision of the Local Autonomy Act, largely as a mitigating measure for city and town mergers. This system was innovative in the history of community policy, as it was positioned for collaboration between administrations and residents for the first time. However, with the flow of New Public Management (NPM), the introduction of the Designated Administrator System through the revision of the Local Autonomy Act in 2003 led to many municipalities adopting community development councils and other local autonomous organizations based on local ordinances. As previously mentioned, this style has now become a burden in some regions.

What Is a Neighborhood Association?

Often the administrative staff, let alone residents, do not clearly understand the distinction between neighborhood associations (self-governing associations) and community development councils (variously named according to the local government), complicating the process of reform in this field.

Let's clarify what neighborhood associations (self-governing associations) are. First, regarding their legal positioning, neighborhood associations are generally regarded as unincorporated community-based organizations. But in line with their substantial nature, these association are interpreted as having the capacity to act as "non-juristic associations" under Article 29 of the Code of Civil Procedure. While most neighborhood associations do not have a legal personality, some do, pursuant to the provision for community-based organizations in Article 262-2 of the Local Autonomy Act, which gives legal personality as needed for the registration of assets. Challenges surrounding authorized community organizations will be discussed later.

The lack of legal basis for neighborhood associations stems from the reaction to the wartime regime, as previously mentioned, but in essence, they are highly public organizations and not merely voluntary groups. In recent years, neighborhood associations have been positioned within many municipalities' Autonomy Basic Ordinance or Community Development Ordinance. The principles are mainly interpreted as follows: ① Neighborhood associations are voluntary organizations created through the residents independent will, and are not organizations with membership mandated by law; ② Religious activities by neighborhood or self-governing associations that align with a specific sect must be excluded; and ③ Neighborhood associations must ensure independence and freedom from specific political parties to protect their members' political beliefs.

Membership in neighborhood associations must remain voluntary, and the associations must not be used for specific political or religious purposes. Some neighborhood associations support local government council candidates from nearby areas or request community shrine membership fees and neighborhood association dues, but these types of activities must be distinguished from those of neighborhood associations.

Incorporating the above, two primary misconceptions surrounding neighborhood associations can be identified. First, although neighborhood associations are voluntary organizations, the notion that they operate without governmental intervention is mistaken. They receive subsidies from the administration, are positioned within local ordinances, and are profoundly public entities. The government has a responsibility to provide guidance and advice to ensure their proper operation. Second, neighborhood associations are not extraterritorial. Providing false reports to the administration constitutes forgery of official documents, while misappropriating or embezzling funds, such as neighborhood association fees, can result in charges of embezzlement in official business. Regrettably, it is not uncommon for residents to dismiss the seriousness of matters concerning association reports or funds. However, meticulous management is essential for general meeting records and accounting.

Similar to the previously mentioned community planning councils, neighborhood associations across the country face numerous challenges today.
The primary issues include,

① Declining membership rate—Residents often do not perceive the benefits of joining their neighborhood association, and instead feel it is a burden. Voices lamenting the lack of representation, especially among younger individuals and women, are frequently heard.
② Volunteer shortages due to the declining birth-rate and aging population—Too many activities and organizational tasks are leading to an absence of volunteers; the extent of voluntary activities is also reaching its limits.
③ Multiple terms of office holders—Office holders tend to remain the same because of the lack of participants, potentially leading to undemocratic management.
④ Financial issues—Budgets are often decided by a select few office holders, and the use of grants and other funds lacks transparency. There is also an observed imbalance in budgets due to insufficient independent financial sources, fixed membership fees, and allocation of funds to specific projects.

Without addressing these myriad challenges, neighborhood associations will likely see an even greater decline in membership and may struggle with their operations in the future. In the worst-case scenario, they may even become the hotbed for misconduct.

Urban Planning Councils

Next, I will clarify the meaning of urban planning councils. As previously mentioned, the prototype of urban planning councils was the regional council under the Local Autonomy Law. Regional councils were established along with the regional-autonomy system through the amendment of the Local Autonomy Act in 2004. With the aim of enriching local self-governments, these councils were designed to create districts, consolidate residents' opinions through regional councils, and place offices to handle local matters. In terms of authority, they serve as a consultation point for mayors on important matters related to the regional autonomy district as defined by ordinance, and have the right to make recommendations to the mayors.

The head of the council must be selected by the mayor from residents in the district, with consideration to ensuring that diverse opinions are properly reflected. In this way, regional councils are closer to citizen assemblies, separate from neighborhood associations, and urban planning councils adhere to this purpose.

Some municipalities may argue that their urban planning councils established based on ordinances are different from the regional councils under the Local Autonomy Law. However, how can municipalities that operate urban planning councils as though they are surrogate neighborhood associations explain the difference? To put it bluntly, it appears that urban planning councils and neighborhood association systems are often confused and misused.

In summary, the various issues surrounding urban planning councils include ① The significance of neighborhood associations and urban planning councils is not understood and their roles not clearly delineated; ② Duplication and conflict between organizations and projects, or a dictatorial operation where one person holds dual roles; ③ The councils serving as proxies for neighborhood associations or becoming event organizations, with residents feeling these are unnecessary layers; and ④ The introduction of the Designated Administrator System further increasing the sense of government irresponsibility and residents' burden, leading to problems such as the ballooning of grants.

Various Regional Management Organizations

In addition to traditional community self-government organizations like neighborhood associations and urban planning councils, various organizations and projects to manage regions have been advocated by different ministries in recent years. Examples include the Ministry of Agriculture, Forestry, and Fisheries' Rural Region Management Organization (Rural RMO) and the Ministry of Land, Infrastructure, Transport and Tourism's Promotion of 'Hometown Village Life Zones' Centered around 'Small Bases.'

The definition of a Rural Region Management Organization (Rural RMO) is an organization that "complements the functions of multiple villages, preserving agricultural land and engaging in economic activities centered around agriculture, in addition to supporting the maintenance of community life." Specifically, it involves

A) Targeting a range that spans multiple villages (e.g., a primary school district).
B) Forming village agreements by multiple villages, agricultural corporations, etc.
C) Collaborating with various regional stakeholders, including self-governing bodies, neighborhood associations, and social welfare councils, to establish councils.
D) Engaging in the three "Preservation of Agricultural Land," "Utilization of Regional Resources," and "Support for Living" projects.

Similarly, "Small Bases" refers to the effort to "connect various dispersed daily life services and regional activities in basic living areas, such as primary school districts, through combining techniques and circulating people, goods, and services, thereby supporting new regional management mechanisms."

Each ministry promotes these projects according to their areas of expertise, but the essence remains the same. It is about gathering organizations, projects, public facilities, and other regional resources, which have decreased in proportion to population decline and financial difficulties, with everyone working together on what the region truly needs.

Local governments and regions are free to adopt any regional management organization or project proposed by each ministry. However, as I will mention later, the prerequisite for adoption is the scrapping and rebuilding of existing organizations and projects. Without this basic sorting, simply introducing new corporations or systems will pile layer upon layer and will ultimately fail.

Local governments and regions must first systematically carry out this most complicated and challenging task.

Flawed Intermediate Support (Community Support & Collaboration Support)

Some municipalities have already set up centers for civic activities, providing intermediate support. From my perspective, however, there are many problematic examples of intermediate support. Broadly speaking, five points can be highlighted.

The first is "the lack of clear delineation between public and private roles." Various groups exist in a community, each engaging in activities, and usually receiving various financial aid from the government. Yet, this financial support is often extended by different municipal departments to various groups without a centralized understanding of which group receives what assistance. Furthermore, financial support is often spent annually just because it has been in the past.

Financial support is part of the intermediate support measures, but in any case, the focus should be on community self-government, citizen self-government, or citizen collaboration. Without first clarifying the public and private division of roles, namely, what roles the administration, the community and its citizens should take on, or what part should be jointly undertaken by the administration and citizens, it will be impossible to determine where assistance should be provided. There are numerous cases where local governments disburse subsidies simply by following precedents, without delegating the division of roles between the public and private sectors. I will elaborate on this later, but when providing intermediate support, it is essential to first investigate the current situation of the region, while organizing the division of roles between the public and private sectors.

The second issue is "understanding the community," which refers to instances where administrative officials carry out projects without understanding what a community is. Basically, there are two types of communities. One is the "regional (geographically-based) community," such as neighborhood associations and town development councils. The other is the "purpose-driven (theme-based) community," which includes NPOs and voluntary citizen activity groups. However, when observing local government community support measures, there are numerous cases where support is given only to NPOs and collaborative projects, without any support provided for regional (geographically-based) communities. Even within the administration, the differences between autonomy, collaboration, and NPO policies are not clarified, and confusion is evident. One prominent example is the Autonomy Basic Ordinance that should define the basics of autonomy, but instead often serves as a collaborative ordinance. In extreme cases, some local governments label it a "town-making ordinance" or merely a "philosophical ordinance." This leaves us clueless as to the purpose of creating such an ordinance. First, just as administrative officials must recognize the difference between neighborhood associations and town development councils, they must clearly define what a community is and what areas should be supported, because specific support measures cannot be implemented without clearly defining these terms and targets.

The third point is the misconception that legalizing community associations will solve community problems. Concerning authorized local community groups, the Ministry of Internal Affairs and Communications' Local Government Strategy 2040 Concept Research Group's Second Report states as follows: "Most local management organizations are voluntary groups without legal personality, and those run by authorized local community groups are rare. In meetings of experts at the Cabinet Office, the merits of legal personality include ① alleviating anxiety regarding the burden on individual representatives, ② expanding the scope of projects through contracts and collaboration with various organizations, and ③ stabilizing the securing of human resources."

From this, it can be seen that some local governments are trying to legalize neighborhood associations as a community policy goal, but in many cases it is doubtful whether the true essence is actually understood. What this really means is that the national government is aiming to legalize local management organizations because the legal basis of local management organizations has remained fragile since the days before World War II. However, legalization itself is not the real goal. The real aim is to strengthen regional governance. Many voluntary local management organizations operate ambiguously, so the expectation is proper management achieved through legalization. The same can be said for the previously mentioned town development councils, but merely creating town development councils or authorized local community groups will not solve community problems. Rather, some groups are becoming more closed due to their legal status and unwelcoming to newcomers. The essential aspect is not legalization, but reviewing the organization and business up until that point, and properly organizing the accounting and other elements. That is what should be done. Without this organization, simply establishing a corporation will not solve community problems.

Local governments seem to avoid this difficult organization, but the entire administration, including the mayor, need to work with residents to undertake such reforms as the reorganization of neighborhood associations.

The fourth issue is the problem of "financial support and human support." There are mainly two types of intermediate support. The most common is financial support through subsidies. However, the reality is that most local governments do not know what to do after uniformly granting funds to NPOs within the municipality. Moreover, there are many cases where funds go to large NPOs capable of operating without subsidies, while smaller projects and groups that really need funding are overlooked. In particular, automatic lump-sum grants calculated based on population ratio and area ratio need to be reviewed. As mentioned in the section on revising expenditures for subsidies and burden payments, fixed subsidies often lead to unnecessary consumption, or in the worst case, embezzlement and misappropriation, with the primary goal being to use up the subsidies. The administration should properly understand what activities the relevant region will carry out in the new fiscal year at the budget formulation stage, and budget the necessary subsidy amount accordingly. Furthermore, there are cases where only federations such as neighborhood associations are eligible for subsidies or as applicants, but those actually carrying out the activities are individual groups or organizations within the region. Such cases where real hardworking people are neither targeted for subsidies nor able to apply must be rectified immediately. This is a matter that can be solved by revising subsidy guidelines, and it is not a difficult issue. A representative example of human support is the "Regional Staff System." Unfortunately, in many cases the system involves administrative officials merely acting as the area's errand runner or on behalf of the secretariat. This kind of financial support or human support cannot be considered genuine support. The real goal of community support is to assist in turning the independent activities of residents into sustainable projects and nurturing organizations able to operate autonomously. I would like local governments to recognize and promote the importance of hosting lectures and training sessions for such human resource development.

The fifth issue is that of "intermediary support organizations." As I have mentioned so far, organizations such as citizen activity centers, which are often intermediary support organizations focused on NPO support, frequently either fail to support local community types or are highly vulnerable. One of the reasons, as I have stated, is the misunderstanding among many administrative staff that the administration should not interfere with community self-government. Additionally, as I noted earlier, most support measures are fiscal support measures provided through subsidies, and support for essential business development and organizational growth is weak.

The administration should not merely hand over community support to intermediary support organizations but should do what it must, such as checking documents and accounts, proposing reorganization plans for neighborhood associations, and more. However, it is essential to skillfully utilize intermediary support organizations for matters that may cause friction if stated directly by the administration, and to actively engage in community self-government.

Regional Reform Procedures

The procedures for regional reform are proportional to those for administrative reform and follow the sequence of ① Regional Diagnosis and Clarification of the Division of Roles between Public and Private Sectors → ② Scrap & Build of Organizations and Initiatives → ③ Formulation of Appropriate Intermediate Support Measures → ④ Proper Monitoring.

Let me explain each stage in detail. The first is "Regional Diagnosis." There are precedents for regional diagnoses, or "community medical records," across the country. Many of them identify the positive aspects and challenges of a community, and some municipalities are conducting workshops accordingly. However, a genuine regional diagnosis must grasp the actual conditions of the region in greater depth, including not only statistical matters like population decline or the percentage of the elderly, but also properly understanding less apparent realities, such as the situation of the socially withdrawn requiring support or people with mobility issues. Is the neighborhood association operated appropriately? What are the most pressing issues in the region? There is also the need to recognize the kinds of organizations that exist, the activities conducted, and the kind of public support provided, as a backdrop to later discussions on public support measures.

Unless this factual understanding is accurately conducted, precise community support cannot be provided. Therefore, this initial regional diagnosis is crucial, akin to the first "inventory of operations" in administrative reform.

There are various methods for conducting a regional diagnosis. Actual field surveys, interviews with relevant parties, or even questionnaire surveys are among them. Distributing and collecting anonymous survey forms from residents have certain advantages like candid responses. It is vital to set survey items that truly reveal the community's realities and residents' consciousness, and not just superficial questionnaires.

Simultaneously, as previously stated, municipalities must organize the division of roles between the public and private sectors within the region. By doing so, examples where the administration has been involved more than expected or instances where support is needed but entirely neglected may emerge. Consolidating overlapping support measures through interdepartmental collaboration can also lead to budgetary efficiency.

Second, "Scrap & Build of Organizations and Initiatives" is crucial. Scrapping organizations and initiatives that lack local support, where participation has dwindled or become superficial, and mitigating the burden on the community are important steps to take. For organizations this includes integrating and reorganizing community councils or neighborhood associations, and further consolidating by field. For example, in child-related fields this means the integration or abolition of organizations conducting similar activities, including children's associations, youth development citizen councils, and community council education subcommittees. In terms of initiatives this refers to the discontinuation of such activities as district dance festivals or sports festivals where participation has decreased. It does not mean doing nothing, but slimming down burdensome organizations and initiatives, and reconstructing those that are genuinely needed.

Of course, an administration cannot unilaterally enforce reorganization, and those involved often make little progress. It is preferable for the administration to take the lead, establishing an impartial third-party organization comprised of experts and collaborating with municipal staff to create a framework. It is also desirable to consider integration and reorganization in collaboration with citizens and groups in the region.

At the same time, it is crucial to consider collaboration with highly public private entities, for instance, post offices, agricultural cooperatives, and private companies. As stated in Chapter 1, private companies and other organizations can be significant partners in future public policy.

Third, the "Formulation of Appropriate Intermediate Support Measures" is necessary. After the above described ① Regional Diagnosis and Clarification of the Division of Roles between Public and Private Sectors and ② Scrap & Build of Organizations and Initiatives, actual community support measures are examined.

Examples include basic support like the creation of appropriate rules or accounting training for community self-governance organizations. Various support measures can also be mentioned, such as human support (community staff system), financial support (grants, contracted expenses), environmental development, information provision, guidance, and talent development.

In regions or activities where support measures are not in place, new implementation is necessary, and with the emergence of new regional challenges comes the need to create new systems.

On the other hand, budget limitations make it is necessary to consolidate existing support measures based on priorities. Even if the support measures continue, it is essential to reconsider whether the grant allocation method is appropriate, and whether the burden ratio of burden money is suitable.

Lastly, there is the issue of "Proper Monitoring." Just like administrative reform, regional reform is not a one-time process but requires continual reassessment. It is desirable to establish intermediate support organizations to facilitate this process. An intermediate support organization does not necessarily mean erecting a grand community activity center or similar facility. As long as the functions and structures for intermediate support are in place, that should be sufficient. A suitable organizational example would include an impartial third-party body capable of objective professional insights, including attorneys (judicial scriveners), certified public accountants (tax accountants), social insurance and labour consultants, financial institutions, NPO specialists, and university professors. It might be acceptable to have such people (excluding secretariat staff) working part-time. Their duties could include ① information collection and provision, ② consultation services, ③ guidance and advice, ④ training and seminars, ⑤ regional diagnosis, and ⑥ collaboration with experts and related institutions, among others.

Furthermore, the intermediate support organizations should ① provide detailed follow-up to the community without a sense of complete reliance on the administration, and ② engage in monitoring from a rational and objective standpoint, even pointing out issues. Both these responsibilities are considered essential.

Conclusion

As previously stated, regional reform is part of administrative management reform. It is a fact, however, that many local governments fail to grasp this concept when communicating with their administrative reform or community affairs departments. The need for community reconstruction is urgent with the onset of the nation's declining population and aging society. Alongside reconstruction, a review of the financial expenditures flowing into these areas is essential to securing the necessary budgets for maintaining future communities. Community breakdown has already begun in various parts of the country. There is not much time left. Not only the departments in charge of administrative reform and community affairs, but all departments related to the region should gather to seriously discuss future community policies.

References

※ Nakata Minoru, Yamasaki Takeo, and Ogiso Youshi, "Regional Revitalization and Neighborhood Associations & Residents' Associations," Local Government Research Company (2012)

※ Ministry of Internal Affairs and Communications, "Local Government Strategy 2040 Vision Study Group Second Report" (2018)

※ Ministry of Agriculture, Forestry and Fisheries website, "Promotion of Rural-Type Regional Management Organizations (Rural RMO) - Community Building for Mutual Support" https://www.maff.go.jp/j/nousin/nrmo/ (accessed in December 2022)

※ Ministry of Land, Infrastructure, Transport, and Tourism website, "Promotion of 'Hometown Village Life Zones' Centered around 'Small Bases'" https://www.mlit.go.jp/kokudoseisaku/chisei/crd_chisei_tk_000021.html (accessed in December 2022)

Afterword

In 2022, NHK's historical drama highlighted the life of Hojo Yoshitoki, the regent who effectively established the structure of the warrior-led Kamakura shogunate. On a personal note, I should humbly mention that, according to family lore, my maternal ancestors are descendants of the Hojo clan who, after the fall of the Kamakura shogunate, took refuge in the western lands of Atsuta Shrine in Owari province and subsequently adopted the surname Yokoi.

The drama portrayed Yoshitoki's efforts to consolidate the fledgling shogunal structure, at times employing military force and autocratic measures to maintain control over the samurai. However, as the story unfolds it becomes evident that mere force alone is insufficient to win the hearts and minds of the warriors. The establishment of just and transparent rules is paramount. This notion is underscored by the enactment of "Goseibai Shikimoku" by Yoshitoki's son, Yasutoki, which is regarded as Japan's first samurai legal code – a fact familiar to any Japanese from their history textbooks.

Not only warriors but people at large harbor grievances when benefits accrue exclusively to particular individuals or groups due to opaque processes and standards not rooted in fairness. This truth, evident in the Kamakura period, remains unchanged nearly 800 years later in the present day.

Every year I receive requests from several local governments to conduct reviews of their administrative operations and revisions of subsidies and charges. During these tasks I often encounter subsidies with completely unclear foundations and procedures. This situation sometimes makes me wonder if these are the municipalities of a modern rule-of-law country like Japan. An administration based on fair rules is a fundamental principle of democracy. I hope that local government heads, councilors, and employees will engrave this principle in their minds and conduct sound local government management.

We would like to continue to support the hard-working local governments and their employees.

March 2023
Edited by:
Koji Yokoyama
Professor of Economics, Shiga University / Director of the Social Collaboration Center

Editor and Author Profile
Koji Yokoyama
Professor, Faculty of Economics, Shiga University / Director of the Center for Social Collaboration

Authors and Contributions
Koji Yokoyama
Professor, Faculty of Economics, Shiga University / Director of the Center for Social Collaboration
(Chapters 1-4, 6, 8, 12-13, 15)

Koji Hirose
Representative Director, County Consulting, Inc. (Chapter 5)

Akiyuki Sannomiya
KKC Information System, Corporation Head of the Municipal DX Promotion Room (Chapter 7)

Kazuo Kondo
Kazuo Kondo Tax Accountant Office, Director (Chapter 9)

Ryota Hirose
Tax Accountants Corporation TACT, Takai Norihiro Accounting Office, Tax Accountant (Chapter 10)

Akihisa Hirata
Nihon Suido Consultants Co.,Ltd, Senior Engineer (Chapter 11)

Taketo Shima
CareerLink Corporation , Managing Executive Officer (Chapter 14)

Translator
Yosuke Morizono
Futurise Consulting, Representative (Responsible for the entire translation)

Theory and Practice of Administrative Reform

March 31, 2024 First edition first printing published

Author : Koji Yokoyama
Publisher : Junko Iwane
Publisher : Sunrise Publishing Co., Ltd.
655-1 Toriimotocho, Hikone City, Shiga Prefecture 522-0004
Printing / binding Sunrise Publishing Co., Ltd.

©YOKOYAMA Koji 2024
ISBN978-4-88325-812-3